Information on Music: A Handbook of Reference Sources in European Languages, Volume I

INFORMATION ON MUSIC:
A HANDBOOK OF REFERENCE SOURCES IN
EUROPEAN LANGUAGES

GUY A. MARCO

Information on Music:

A Handbook of

Reference Sources

in European Languages

Volume I, Basic and Universal Sources

By

GUY A. MARCO

With the assistance of Sharon Paugh Ferris

Foreword by James Coover
Professor of Music and Music Librarian,
State University of New York, Buffalo

LIBRARIES UNLIMITED, INC., Littleton, Colo.

1975

LIBRARIES UNLIMITED, INC.
P.O. Box 263
Littleton, Colorado 80120

Library of Congress Cataloging in Publication Data

Marco, Guy A
    Information on music.   146235

    Includes indexes.
    CONTENTS: v. 1. Basic and universal sources.
    1. Music--Bibliography. 2. Music--Discography--
Bibliography. 3. Bibliography--Bibliography--Music.
I. Ferris, Sharon Paugh. II. Title.
ML113.M33   016.78   74-32132
ISBN 0-87287-096-0

FOREWORD

Anyone who enjoys poking around in the neglected corners of music literature, who is intrigued by the old and now-forgotten, must have a special fondness for Carl Ferdinand Becker's attempt at a complete bibliography of music literature, his *Darstellung* of 1836 (Supplement 1839; see Marco number 0421). Those corners yield many delights, for there is hardly a page in the book that does not reveal an obscure work that piques the imagination, and hardly one of Becker's annotations that does not whet the reader's curiosity.

Becker's attempt to present a *complete* bibliography attests to that seemingly irresistible urge in man to comprehend all the facts and ideas of his intellectual life—to comprehend them, control them, to order them for his use. Before Becker there were others with the same hopes—most notably Adlung (Marco 0212), Forkel (Marco 0217), and Lichtenthal (Marco 0221)—but there were none later. By the mid-nineteenth century the output of the world's printing presses made Becker's goal of "all" clearly unattainable, at least for a lone bibliographer. Eitner may have been impelled by that old urge when he launched his monumental *Quellen-Lexikon* (Marco 0431) in 1898, but from Becker's time on, the aim of comprehensiveness had to be tailored to more specific topics within music, or to a nation, a language, or a period of time.

The need—the urge—did not go away, of course. In our time we attempt to assuage it, not through the work of individuals, but through large, cooperative, sometimes automated, projects such as RISM (Marco 0419, 0255), RILM (Marco 0260), RIdIM (Marco p. 32), and the *National Union Catalogue* (Marco 0239). These efforts, as well as Becker's, are spiritually linked to classical antecedents (see Marco's section "Historical Sources" in Chapter 1, "The Language of Music"), for the idea of man controlling knowledge is as old as intelligent man himself. The only real innovations down through history have been in methods.

Reading Becker can be worrisome, too. The enormous amount of material that existed for him to list 150 years ago suggests the amount requiring bibliographical controls today. Much of what exists remains available to us only with difficulty (numerous Ph.D. dissertations consist of the bringing together of fugitive materials from far-flung sources), and if history is to be believed, the very existence of masses of musical materials is still unknown (as the recent discoveries of Robbins Landon and others have shown).

That awesome backlog, however, is but part of our problem, for faster than we recover the old we invent the new. The phenomenon of Rock, in a few frantic years, has generated thousands of recordings and printed scores and a flood of books and journal articles. The challenges to bibliographical comprehension are enormous—and not all conventional. For Rock and much avant-garde music the performance is the composition, the recording its publication. And how does one make a thematic catalog of the works of John Cage or Anestis Logothetis? Or determine the "Urtext" (a word that used to offer some comfort) of Haubenstock-Ramati's *Credentials*?

New tools and techniques will have to be created for the new, even though the old still wants for more and better controls. An inventory of those needed controls might suggest impoverishment, but that is far from the truth. In sheer numbers music probably enjoys as many reference sources as most subjects. It is only when those sources are subdivided into categories—one for books and journals, one for scores, another for recordings—that one notices a lack of depth. Nevertheless, the number of those sources is sufficient to have induced the production of several guides to guides—Winchell-like compilations, some of which, like Marco's present work, are annotated—to help musicians locate needed information. We have been grateful for and have exploited to their fullest Duckles' *Music Reference and Research Materials* (Marco 0216), Spiess's *Historical Musicology* (Marco, Vol. 3), Watanabe's *Introduction to Music Research* (Marco 0225), and others. Of such tools there are never enough, and the quantity of materials that can be introduced into any one such compilation admits of great variety.

Selecting the most useful works to include in this guide was, of course, Marco's first job; correlating them was his second. The aim is still comprehensiveness, but it is a comprehensiveness different from that sought by Becker. Here it is a desire to fulfill all or most of the demands that will be placed on the finished work while, for the sake of clarity, listing the fewest number of reference tools needed to achieve that goal.

Selection involves deciding what is and what is not a reference tool and how each item selected is to be correlated with others. In his modest introduction, Marco touches casually upon these processes and graciously avoids recounting in detail the thorny problems involved in such decisions. There must have been many nettlesome questions like these to be answered:

Should a dictionary of nineteenth century musicians that contains entries for many obscure persons be included despite its numerous flaws? Should a certain periodical index that extends—but only slightly—the coverage of several others be allowed entrance? Should one catalog that is rich in bibliographical and historical detail be offered when another, without those details, covers the same ground and is more up to date by 15 years? Should a slight and superficial book, which is, however, the only one of its kind, be enshrined in these pages? And where should this library catalog of operas in manuscript be listed—under the name of the library, under "Manuscripts," or under "Operas"? Does a rich source of pre-1800 materials such as Eitner's *Quellen-Lexikon* belong in the section on pre-1800 sources or with the dictionaries?

Among the thousands of items Marco considered for inclusion and the hundreds that he ultimately chose, every bibliographer knows that there were distressingly few whose character was categorical and that did not pose such dilemmas. Becker's job was easier!

In this, the first of six welcome volumes, Marco has answered the question of selection from a clear and informed view of the potential user's needs. He brings to that task a critical acumen matured through long years of experience with those users. And by skillful arrangement and generous, informative summaries he reveals the utility of the works cited and correlates them among the various sections and among the six volumes. Integrated throughout are many general reference works that are important to music research. Not everyone will agree completely with what he has left out, what he has included, or with all of the locations he has chosen for the material he does include. But such is the fate of any bibliographer who dares to labor with this sprawling literature, which lends itself less readily to scientific than to artful organization (an organization that seems appropriate, somehow).

Marco's goal is not to list *all* reference sources—thank goodness—but there are plenty of items here, as in Becker, that will catch the imagination and whet the curiosity of the users, most of whom will wish, as I do, that the book had been available long ago.

James Coover
Buffalo, New York

To Scott Goldthwaite, *primus motor*

ACKNOWLEDGMENTS

Research for this volume was pursued in a number of libraries, with the cooperation and assistance of several librarians: Northwestern University, School of Music Library (Don Roberts); Newberry Library (Bernard Wilson); Ohio State University, School of Music Library (Olga Buth); Kent State University, Music Library (Desiree de Charms); and Library of Congress, Music Division (Don Leavitt, William Lichtenwanger, Edward Waters). Vincent Duckles has offered information, advice, and support. James Coover read the manuscript and improved it substantially through his criticisms and suggestions. Two graduate assistants were involved in checking and searching: Cheryl Anson and Hwi-Sook Koh. Valerie Dueber prepared and typed the index, from barely comprehensible entries on cards and scraps. Sharon Paugh Ferris was chief indexer, verifier, coordinator, and detective. My warmest thanks to all these fine colleagues.

Special gratefulness is directed to Bohdan Wynar, who encouraged this work over many years and who patiently changed his publication plans to suit my own irresponsibility about deadlines.

TABLE OF CONTENTS

"What can we reason but from what we know?"

INTRODUCTION

Find a point where two intellectual worlds touch, and you will find a scholar in search of a bibliographer. For the expert is an expert because of his isolation, which means that he becomes an amateur in confrontation with fields not his own. No one is more conscious of this fact than a resident in that vast galactic complex called "music": where the opera singer is a stranger to the folk singer, the conductor cannot read pre-Bach notation, and the medievalist does not recognize the names of today's composers. The present work is offered to musicians in the hope of harmonizing some of their diverse spheres, at least on the level of factuality. It is a handbook of information sources that the expert, within his own tight subject, will not require—but that that same expert could find to be timesaving when he strays outside the compound. I hope it will also serve some of the purposes of reference librarians, particularly those who face frequent inquiries of an esoteric nature.

There is a fine listing of information materials in music by Vincent Duckles, entitled *Music Reference and Research Materials* (3d ed., Free Press, 1974). I have sought to correlate my efforts with those of Dr. Duckles, avoiding unneeded duplication of content in several areas, and bringing out certain features of the books he cites which I thought could use particular emphasis. I have also tried to bring together specifically musical materials and more general works into what is intended to be a unified perspective toward the totality of available facts.

Excellence, convenience, and uniqueness have been my essential criteria for inclusion. These criteria do tend to interflow, however, so I have endeavored to approach them in this manner: the user's convenience in locating information is best served if a single source for each type of information can be identified. Where several admirable sources exist, vis-à-vis a given type of information (say, facts about contemporary jazz musicians), my decision on whether to list one or several has been centered on the amount of overlapping among them. If one book can serve the purpose, I have not thought it desirable to present the names of a dozen. If three are needed to cover a topic, I have mentioned them and their respective utilities.

One aspect of convenience is linguistic congruence. I have posited a user who is able to draw facts from books in French or German as well as English, and those languages account for the bulk of inclusions. But it must be acknowledged that significant writing on a great many musical topics is found in other languages, and if the most essential information sources for certain subjects happen to be in tongues that are less widely known, those sources are cited. As might be expected, the principal sources in nationalistic topics tend to be in the native language, so Volume II is notably polyglot.

My limitation to works in European languages (arbitrarily excluding Turkish) should not be seen as an omission of non-European topics. Writings about the music of Asia and Africa will be found, as well as bibliographical apparatus from those nations, insofar as such materials are themselves written in a European language.

Form of presentation generally follows that of the Library of Congress; indeed, I have taken my entries verbatim from LC cards with only slight modifications. LC classmarks are given except in a very few cases.

Several bibliographic source-works are cited regularly in shortened style:

ARBA *American Reference Books Annual* (1970, 1971, 1972, 1973, 1974). Littleton, Colo.: Libraries Unlimited, 1970– .

Duckles 67 Vincent Duckles, *Music Reference and Research Materials.* 2d ed. New York: Free Press, 1967.

Duckles 74 Ibid., 3d ed., 1974.

Winchell 67 Constance Winchell, *Guide to Reference Books.* 8th ed. Chicago: American Library Association, 1967. Supplements covering 1965/66, 1967/68, 1969/70.

These source-works have numbered items; the appropriate number after the source is usually self-explanatory—but notice that Winchell's supplement numbers begin with the number of the supplement (Winchell67–2BH100 = item BH100 in the second supplement, 1967/68). ARBA 1970 did not have item numbers, so citations thereto are given by page only.

Guy A. Marco, Dean
School of Library Science
Kent State University

CHAPTER 1

THE LANGUAGE OF MUSIC

A word or phrase dropped by a composer into his score can be troublesome to interpret, particularly if a few hundred years have elapsed since he made his inscriptions. And verbalisms that are used in a single time-place situation for describing some musical instrument or style may be impenetrable to readers living outside the same context. Music dictionaries are the logical places to check for such terms, but the larger general dictionaries in various languages must not be overlooked. And for problematic terms, it may be necessary to examine treatises on "interpretation" which will set forth a range of options. But let us begin with basics.

MOST USEFUL DICTIONARIES OF TERMS

0001 Adams, John Stowell. **Adams' New Musical Dictionary of Fifteen Thousand Technical Words, Phrases, Abbreviations, Initials, and Signs . . . in Nearly Fifty Ancient and Modern Languages . . .** 2d ed. New York: Hamilton S. Gordon, c1893. (1st ed. c1865). 271p. ML108 A214

Terms are defined in just a few words. Most of them are actually in common languages, but coverage of Welsh, Gaelic, Greek, and some Asiatic tongues would be hard to find elsewhere.

0002 Apel, Willi. **Harvard Dictionary of Music.** 2d ed. Cambridge, Mass.: Belknap Press of Harvard University Press, 1969. (1st ed. c1944). xv, 935p. ML100 A64 1969

Duckles 67–199 (for 1st ed.); Duckles 74–275; Winchell 67–3BH18; ARBA 70–II, 23

The standard American dictionary, including definitions and brief articles on all topics other than biographical. With few exceptions, terms are in English, French, German, Italian, Spanish, Latin, and Greek. One advantage Harvard has over the competition is the practice of citing books and articles that will give more background on the term or topic; however, this bibliographic coverage is uneven. Another strength is the great number of diagrams, drawings, and musical examples (no photographs, though). Scholarship is generally sound—an international group of authorities contributed in various subject areas. The searcher for terms should note that many are buried in topical articles or mentioned in discussions of related expressions, without cross references. In this connection, the following little supplement will be useful: *Hidden Terms in the Harvard Dictionary*, by Mary Paterson and Susanne Ritari (unpublished paper, Kent State University, School of Library Science, 1973), 77p.

1

0003   Baker, Theodore. **Dictionary of Musical Terms ... with a Supplement Containing an English-Italian Vocabulary for Composers.** 21st ed. New York: G. Schirmer, 1923. (1st ed. c1895). 257p. Reprint— New York: AMS Press. ML108 B165
        Duckles 67–201; Duckles 74–277; Winchell 67–BH68
Some 9,000 terms, plus some useful features: list of abbreviations of common expressions, accentuation of foreign words, illustrations of unusual signs. Note the appendix of newer terms. Limited to English, French, German, Italian, Latin, and Greek.

0004   Duncan, Edmondstone. **Encyclopedia of Musical Terms, Defining Some 20,000 Words and Phrases in All Languages ...** New York: G. Schirmer; Boston: Boston Music Company, 1914. 455p. ML108 D87
Between 13,000 and 14,000 terms would seem to be a more accurate estimate. Very good in German, and for unusual English expressions (note, for instance, the patient tabulation of compound words; e.g., there are 51 entries beginning with "double-").

0005   Hiles, John. **A Complete and Comprehensive Dictionary of 12,500 Italian, French, German, English, and Other Musical Terms ...** 12th ed. London: F. Pitman Hart, n.d. (1st ed. 1871). ML108 H45
Appears to contain closer to 9,000 terms. Very brief definitions; hardly any illustrations.

0006   Smith, William James. **A Dictionary of Musical Terms in Four Languages.** London: Hutchinson, 1961. 195p. ML108 S64 D5
        Duckles 67–220; Duckles 74–305;
Useful for its columnar arrangement of entries by languages, which simplifies the search for equivalencies. The languages are English, French, German, and Italian.

0007   Stainer, Sir John, and William Alexander Barrett. **Stainer and Barrett's Dictionary of Musical Terms ...** New and rev. ed. London: Novello, 1898. (1st ed. 1876). Reissued, 1912. Reprint—Hildesheim: Georg Olms, 1970. 464p. ML108 S78
        Duckles 67–221; Duckles 74–306;
Around 11,000 terms, briefly defined. Useful for Scottish, Hebrew, Russian, Spanish, and Arabic entries.

0008   Torrellas, A. Albert. **Diccionario enciclopédico de la música.** Dirección general: A. Albert Torellas. Barcelona: Central Catalana de Publicaciones, 1947-52. 4v. ML100 D485
        Duckles 67–13; Duckles 74–12
The first volume is a dictionary of some 10,000 terms, with special strength in Middle East and Asiatic vocabularies. Definitions are all in Spanish, without equivalents in other languages. Many good illustrations, particularly for notational elements.

0009   Vannes, René. **Essai de terminologie musicale** . . . Thann: "Alsatia,"
        c1925. xii, 230p. ML106 V18
            Duckles 67–226; Duckles 74–312; Winchell 67–BH72
        With more than 15,000 terms, this seems to be the most comprehen-
sive dictionary. It covers Italian, Spanish, Portuguese, French, English,
German, Latin, and Greek; definitions are in French, with equivalents in
other languages.

0010   Wotton, Tom. **Dictionary of Foreign Musical Terms and Handbook
        of Orchestral Instruments**. Leipzig: Breitkopf & Härtel, 1907. vi,
        226p. ML108 W78
            Duckles 67–227; Duckles 74–313; ARBA 74–1081
        About 9,000 terms, many of which are not found elsewhere.

        Although much duplication is evident among these ten dictionaries,
the number of terms found in just one or two of them is substantial. Looking
just at Adams, Apel, and Duncan, for example, we see "galiambus" in Adams
only, "gallant style" in Apel only, "gassatio" in Duncan only. Adams appears
to have more of these single appearances than do the others.
        While these works identify more than 25,000 terms, they still need
to be supplemented. They lack sufficient attention to less familiar languages,
and they do not give full treatment to obsolete words and non-current
spellings. These and other aspects of musical terminology are explored in the
group that follows.

0011   **Webster's New International Dictionary of the English Language**. 2d
        ed. Springfield, Mass.: Merriam, 1934. 3194p. PE1625 W3 1934
            Winchell 67–AE7
        "Webster 2" (or "W2") defined more than 600,000 words in its
1934 manifestation, and gradually added another 100,000 through the
addenda of later printings. With more entries than any other English
dictionary, this work gives ample coverage of musical expressions, with
particular value in Greek terms and obsolete variants. A unique feature is the
separate grouping of obscure words at the bottom of each page, under a
dividing line.

0012   **Webster's Third New International Dictionary of the English
        Language** . . . Springfield, Mass.: Merriam, 1961. 2662p. PE1625
        W36 1961
            Winchell 67–AE8
        For musical purposes, the third edition ("W3") is less important
than the second. While it does bring in many new terms—e.g., "percussion
stop"—it drops many more. There are some 450,000 entries, of which
100,000 are said to be new, so the toll of archaic and obscure words is
obvious.

0013   **Funk & Wagnalls New Standard Dictionary of the English Lan-
        guage** . . . New York: Funk & Wagnalls, 1913. 2816p. PE1625 S7
        1913
            Winchell 67–AE6

Another fine source for older words and Greek terms. Each printing since 1913 has made changes, but there has not been a totally new edition, which is probably for the best.

Notice that Webster gives the different definitions of a term in historical order. While other dictionaries give the current definition first, in W2 and W3 this will appear last. Another caution regards identification of the book in hand: since there are many other dictionaries coincidentally named "Webster," we must be sure it is actually W2 or W3 we are using (title page should correspond with wordage above). Likewise with F&W–it is only the title given at 0013 that is worth looking at.

Some musical entries not in the Apel Harvard Dictionary but found in one or more of these general dictionaries are: "cathedral chimes" (metal tubes struck with a mallet; their sound resembles distant church bells) in W2 and W3; "heptadecad" (24 tones formed of seven decads each having for a tonic one of the notes of a given heptad) in F&W; "cyclic chorus" in W2 and W3; "tonic minor" in W2 and F&W; "querester" below the line among obsolete variants in W2.

Aside from mere inclusion, we are concerned with the extent of information provided. Although all three general dictionaries and Apel include entries for "tonic sol-fa," the only diagram of the system appears in F&W, and the only example of a real melody written out in syllables is in W2. But Apel is more rewarding in some other ways–e.g., a list of references.

Certain dictionaries are basically historical:

0014 **Oxford English Dictionary**. Oxford: Clarendon Press, 1888-1933. PE1625 M7
Winchell 67–AE20
Various titles, and printings of differing numbers of volumes, with supplements. "OED" is a historical lexicon of the language, whose "purpose is to show the history of every word included from the date of its introduction into the language, giving differences in meaning, spelling, pronunciation, usage, etc., at different periods of the last 800 years" (Winchell). It has a vocabulary of 414,825 words, illustrated by 1,827,306 quotations. Anyone studying British music or British writers on music will find OED extremely helpful in catching exact meanings and connotations. And, of course, there are words that are found only in OED (such as "music demy") or other historical dictionaries ... of which two others are particularly important in our context:

0015 **Dictionary of American English on Historical Principles**. Chicago: University of Chicago Press, 1936-44. 4v. 2552p. PE2835 C72
Winchell 67–AE80

0016 **Dictionary of Americanisms on Historical Principles**. Chicago: University of Chicago Press, 1951. 1946p. PE2835 D5
Winchell 67–AE81
These two complementary works are essential for investigation of the American musical idiom, which is a weak field in the standard musical

reference books. While 0015 is more comprehensive, 0016 is illustrated and also more recent. We find the world of folk and country music well displayed: e.g., "cornstalk fiddle" is defined in 0015 and 0016 (with a drawing in the latter), but is not found in Apel or the other music dictionaries examined. Often an item that is covered by a musical source will get a more thorough—indeed, more reliable—treatment in a general historical dictionary. For instance, Apel says the "Boston" was a kind of waltz "hardly known in America" but "used in Europe . . . after World War I." However, 0016 gives a number of quotes indicating that the Boston was familiar to American writers as early as 1879.

Other bits of musical Americana can be discovered in various regional, dialect and slang dictionaries (mentioned in Winchell), of which just one example is offered here:

0017   Wentworth, Harold, and S. B. Flexner. **Dictionary of American Slang**. Supplemental ed. New York: Crowell, 1967. 718p. PE3729 U5 W4
　　　　Winchell 67—AE72
This is a good hunting ground for hip and rock terms, as well as for some of the older swing and bop language.

DICTIONARIES USEFUL FOR CERTAIN LANGUAGES

Words in languages other than English, especially those not in the major European tongues, often require the use of general national dictionaries. There are equivalents of Webster or F&W in every country; these can be located as needed through Winchell or ARBA. The most thorough coverage is found in the monolingual dictionaries (e.g., the eight-volume opus issued by the Czech Academy, cited by Winchell at AE172), but naturally these are troublesome to use unless one knows a fair amount of the language. Bilingual dictionaries are less satisfactory; they tend to resemble our desk dictionaries rather than our unabridged giants.

In many languages we have specialized music dictionaries. Purely for term identification, items 0001-0010 will take care of most searches in English, French, German, Italian, or Latin. But for older words in those languages, and for words in other languages, the titles that follow will be useful. I have tried to select dictionaries that give equivalents in a more common language, in addition to a definition in the language of the dictionary itself: that is, a book that translates a Latvian term into French seems more widely useful than one that simply defines it in Latvian.

Czech

0018   Barvík, Miroslav. **Stručný hudební slovník**. 5., přeprac. a doplněné vyd., 1. v SNKLHU. Praha: Státní nakl. krásné literatury, hudby a umění, 1960. 415p. ML100 B27

While definitions are in Czech, sometimes an equivalent is given in a more common language (e.g., "maly buben" as "tamburo piccolo"). There is also an illustrated section at the end through which a number of terms can be visually identified.

0019   Válek, Jiří. **Italské hudebnì názvosloví.** 1. vyd. Praha: Panton, 1966. 147p. ML108 V17

Not so many terms as in 0018, but more widely useful since one section of the book translates them into Italian; the other half of the dictionary goes from Italian to Czech.

Danish

0020   **Munksgaards musik leksikon.** Overs. fra fransk og bearb. af Jorgen Praem. København: Munksgaard; Odense: Skandinavisk bogforlag, 1965. 269p. ML100 E483

May be used as a supplementary source to 0021; some terms are identifiable through the illustrations.

0021   Panum, Hortense, and William Behrend. **Illustreret musikleksikon.** Rev. ed. København: Aschehoug, 1940. (1st ed. 1916). 735p. ML100 P16 I5

Duckles 67–35; Duckles 74–41

Many Danish terms are presented with their equivalents in German and/or Italian.

Dutch

0022   **Elsevier's Dictionary of Cinema, Sound, and Music, in Six Languages: English/American, French, Spanish, Italian, Dutch, and German.** Compiled and arr. on an English alphabetical base by W. E. Clason. Amsterdam; New York: Elsevier Publishing Co., 1956. 948p. (Elsevier's multilingual dictionaries). TR847 E4

Duckles 67–207; Duckles 74–285

While this is a polyglot gathering, its principal worth lies in coverage of Dutch expressions that are shown with equivalents from the other languages. However, only 3,213 terms are included; and of those the majority are not musical. Preface states that musical definitions were largely drawn from the *Dictionary of Music*, by Robert Illing (Baltimore: Penguin, 1956).

0023   Gerigk, Herbert. **Woordenboek der muziek.** Nederlandse bewerking Hennie Schouten. Amsterdam: A. J. G. Strengholt, 1970. 200p. ML108 G372

Many Dutch terms are translated into French, German, or Italian; others can be identified through pictures.

English

0024 Carter, Henry Holland. **A Dictionary of Middle English Musical Terms.** Edited by George B. Gerhard and others. Bloomington: Indiana University Press, 1961. Reprint—New York: Kraus, 1968. xv, 655p. (Indiana University humanities series, no. 45) AS36 I385 #45
       Duckles 67—205; Duckles 74—281
       Definitions and quotations from original sources.

0025 Jones, Robert C. **A Glossary of Theoretical Terms Used in Selected Writings in English about Twentieth-Century Music.** Doctoral dissertation, State University of Iowa, 1965. xi, 367p. (Summary in *Dissertation Abstracts*, 26-10, 6089-90).
       Considers old terms with new meanings, terms borrowed from other fields, and new terms. Vocabulary chosen from theoretical words judged to be most influential. Signs and symbols are included.

0026 Padelford, Frederick Morgan. **Old English Musical Terms.** Bonn: P. Hanstein, 1899. xii, 112p. (Bonner Beiträge zur Anglistik, no. 4). ML108 P374
       Duckles 67—215; Duckles 74—296
       Definitions drawn from many old vocabularies, which are carefully identified.

0027 Pulver, Jeffrey. **A Dictionary of Old English Music and Musical Instruments.** London: Kegan Paul; New York: E. P. Dutton, 1923. vi, 247p. ML100 P95
       Duckles 67—216; Duckles 74—297
       Long, historical definitions of some 500 terms used in Elizabethan period. Citations of primary sources; ten plates.

Flemish

Some Flemish terms are included in the glossary of Max Möller's *Violin Makers of the Low Countries*, to be found in Volume III of the present work. Duckles 67—181; Duckles 74—250

German

0028 **Langenscheidts Fachwörterbuch: Musik; Englisch-Deutsch, Deutsch-Englisch.** Von Horst Leuchtmann und Philippine Schick. 1. Aufl. Berlin: Langenscheidt, 1964. 359p. ML108 L3
       Duckles 74—293
       Strong in parts of instruments (e.g., Bogen Schraubenkopf, a bow cap), many of which are among the numerous illustrations. Self-evident cognates are omitted.

Hungarian

0029   Böhm, László. **Zenei műszoótár:** magyarázatokkal, kottapéldákkal, táblázatokkal és hangjegyírás-útmutatóval. Bőv. és átdolg. kiad. Budapest: Zeneműkiadó Vállalat, 1961. (1st ed. 1952). 347p. ML108 B57 Z4 1961
    Terms only. Many Hungarian expressions are translated into Italian or other common languages. Pictures help to identify items for which no equivalent appears.

Indic

0030   Sambamoorthy, P. **A Dictionary of South Indian Music and Musicians.** Madras: Indian Publishing House, 1952– (in progress). ML106 I5 S3
        Duckles 67–108; Duckles 74–142
    Three volumes have appeared, through letter N. Technical terms, forms, operas, instruments, ragas, talas; also biographical entries.

Latin

See items 0049-0053.

Latvian

0031   Albina, Diāna. **Mūzikas terminu vārdnīca.** Redigējis J. Līcītis. Rīgà: Latvijas valsts izdevnieciba, 1962. 303p. ML108 A4
        Duckles 74–274
    In addition to Latvian definitions, terms often receive translation into French, German, or Italian. Illustrations help to understand others.

Norwegian

0032   Gaukstad, Øystein. **Gyldendals musikkleksikon.** Oslo: Gyldendal, 1962. 229p. (Fakkel-bøkene, F35). ML100 G18 G9
    While most terms are defined in Norwegian only, some have equivalents in French, German, or Italian.

Polish

0033   Habela, Jerzy. **Słowniczek muzyczny.** Wyd. 7., zmienione i poszer- zone. Krakow: Polskie Wydawn. Muzyczne, 1969. (1st ed. 1965). 222p. (Biblioteka Słuchacza Koncertowego. Seria Wprowadzajaca, t. 1). ML108 H12 1969.
    A term dictionary with about 2,000 entries. Polish words are usually defined in Polish only, but in some cases there are equivalents in French, German, Latin, or Italian. Pictures are not numerous, but those included are helpful for catching the vocabulary of music notation and musical instruments.

0034   **Mala encyklopedia muzyki.** Redaktor naczelny Stefan Śledziński.
Wyd. 1. Warszawa, Państwowe Wydawn. Naukowe, 1968. 1269p.
ML100 M18
Duckles 74—44
Based on a work of the same title by the late Jozef Reiss. Polish
words are defined in Polish only, but there are enough illustrations to make
identifications possible for many of them. A list of abbreviations, in Polish
and other languages, is a notable feature.

Russian

0035   Katayen, Lelia. **Russian-English Dictionary of Musical Terms.** By
Lelia Katayen and Val Telberg. New York: Telberg Book Corp.,
1965. 125p. ML108 K33
Duckles 67—211; Duckles 74—291; Winchell 67—1BH16
The only source for English translations of Russian terms. Does not
have an English-Russian section.

0036   Dolzhanskiĭ, Aleksandr Naumovich.   **Kratkiĭ muzikal'nyi slovar'.**
Izd. 5. Leningrad: Muzyka, 1966. (1st ed. 1952). ML100 D7 1966
Duckles 67—206 (for 3rd ed.); Duckles 74—283
While 0035 will serve most purposes, for persons who read English,
this item and the two that follow add to the range. They are all monolingual,
but they are amply illustrated so that one can match words with notational
elements, parts of instruments, etc.

0037   **Entsiklopedicheskii muzykal'nyi slovar'.** Avtor'i-sostaviteli B. S.
Shteinpress i I. M. Iampol'skii. Izd. 2-e., ispr. i dop. Moskva:
Sovetskaiia Entsiklopediia, 1966. (1st ed. 1959). 631p. ML100 E58
1966
Duckles 67—21 (for 1st ed.)
Best for pictures of instruments, with all parts labelled, and for a
two-page list of Russian abbreviations. Definitions of Russian terms are given
only in Russian.

0038   Ostrovskii, Aron L'vovich. **Sputnik muzikanta.** Izd. 2. Leningrad:
Muzyka, 1969. (1st ed. 1964). 400p. ML100 O84 1969
Covers notation, instruments, and theoretical vocabulary. Meanings
of many terms can be inferred from the labelled illustrations, but no
translations are given.

Slovenian

0039   Škerjanc, Lucijan Marija. **Glasbeni slovarček.** V Ljubljani: Mladinska
knj., 1962. 241p. ML105 S6
Definitions are in Slovenian only, but some pictures help with
identification, especially of instruments.

Spanish

0040   Bobillier, Marie. **Diccionario de la música** . . . Barcelona: J. Gil, 1946. 548p.

        Duckles 67–203; Duckles 74–278

        A translation from the author's *Dictionnaire pratique* . . . 2d ed. (Paris: A. Colin, 1930). The original and translation appeared under Bobillier's pseudonym, Michel Brenet. The Spanish version has had an infusion of Spanish terms, many of which are not to be found in 0041, 0042, or 0043. While definitions are given in Spanish, without equivalents, there are many helpful illustrations. And for those who can understand enough Spanish, the definitions are extremely informative.

0041   Pedrell, Felipe. **Diccionario técnico de la música.** 2d ed. Barcelona: Isidro Torres Oriol, 1899. (1st ed. 1894). 529p. ML108 P374

        More than 11,000 terms in Spanish, Italian, Latin, French, German, and English, with some cross-referencing among languages.

0042   Pich Santasusana, Juan. **Enciclopedia de la música.** 1. ed. Barcelona: De Gassó Hnos., 1960. 374p. ML100 P52

        Many illustrations aid in identifying Spanish terms, which are defined only in Spanish.

0043   Sardá, Antonio. **Léxico tecnológico musical en varios idiomas** . . . Madrid: Unión Musical Española, c1929. 293p. ML108 S2

        Some definitions are in Spanish only, but in many entries there are equivalents in various languages, including Greek, Hebrew, Dutch, Hungarian, and "Yankee." Pictures are plentiful, especially for showing notational elements.

Swedish

0044   Brodin, Gereon. **Musik ordboken.** 2. utökade och omarbetade uppl. Stockholm: Forum, 1961. 265p. ML100 B85 1961

        Terms are defined in Swedish only; illustrations help to understand some of them. No Swedish dictionary has been checked that is satisfactory from the viewpoint of one who cannot read that language.

0045   Walin, S. "Musikinstrumenttermer i äldre svenska lexikon." *Svensk Tidskrift för Musikforskning,* 30 (1948), 5-40; 31 (1949), 5-82

        A historical dictionary, on the order of 0024, praised by Coover for its "scope, thoroughness, and over-all excellence," and acclaimed as "an exemplar of the type of studies which are needed in this field" (0048, xvii).

AUXILIARY WORKS

    Some books are useful for the assistance they give us in utilization of other works. A basic aid is this guide to abbreviations:

0046   Schaal, Richard. **Abkürzungen in der Musik-Terminologie**: **Eine Übersicht**. 1st ed. Wilhelmshaven: Heinrichshofen, 1969. 165p. ML108 S32

Duckles 74–300

Includes abbreviations, acronyms, standard citations of common journals, standard citations for major musicological works and collected editions of music. Abbreviations of terms in French, German, and Italian. Some of the equivalencies will seem peculiar to American readers; e.g., not many would guess that DE = Denver Public Library.

Special studies of types of terms are used by scholars trying to get at very exact linguistic intentions of early writers on music. A distinguished effort of this genre is:

0047   Eggebrecht, Hans Heinrich. **Studien zur musikalischen Terminologie**. Mainz, Verlag der Akademie der Wissenschaften und der Literatur; in Kommission bei F. Steiner. Wiesbaden, 1955. 131p. (Akademie der Wissenschaften und der Literatur. Abhandlungen der geistes- und sozialwissenschaftlichen Klasse, Jahrg. 1955, Nr. 10). AS182 M232 1955 Nr.10

Compares treatment of 62 terms by early theorists and lexicographers. Among the terms: Akkord, Canon, Cantilena, Harmonia, Modulation, Ricercar, Tempo. Eggebrecht also began issuing, in 1972, a series of detailed articles on individual terms: the *Handwörterbuch der musikalischen Terminologie* (Wiesbaden: Franz Steiner, 1972–). Various scholars are contributing.

This is an opportune point for citing the outstanding bibliographic treatment of music dictionaries:

0048   Coover, James B. **Music Lexicography**. 3rd ed. Carlisle, Pa.: Carlisle Books, 1971. (1st ed. 1952). xxxix, 175p. ML128 D5 C6 1971

Duckles 67–1327 (for 2d ed.); Duckles 74–1846

In addition to his annotated list of 1,801 dictionaries (which encompasses biographical as well as terminological writings), Coover offers some excellent supplementary material: discussions of the gap in dictionary publishing after Tinctoris, comparisons among the three early eighteenth century lexicons (Brossard, Grassineau, and *Short Explication*), lists of treatises with appended glossaries, lists of early non-musical dictionaries containing musical terms, and chronological summaries.

HISTORICAL SOURCES

For access to the musical vocabulary of earlier centuries, there is a block of useful material. Much of it exists only in Greek or Latin, and may be available only in large research libraries; but a fair portion of this terminological heritage has been reprinted and/or translated.

According to an article on "Lexika der Musik" in *Musik in Geschichte und Gegenwart* (0058), the oldest endeavors at defining musical terms appeared in Greek antiquity, incorporated in more general dictionaries. Apel (0002) begins his account of music dictionaries somewhat later: "Some music entries are found in such early dictionaries as the 10th-cent. *Kitab al-Aghani al-Kabir* ... and the *Dictionarius metricus* ascribed to J. de Garlandia ... from the early 13th century." Terms were dealt with in one way or another by various mediaeval writers as well—e.g., Boethius (d.524), Cassiodorus (479-575), Isidore of Seville (565-636), and indeed many of the patristic writings are relevant.

It seems that the earliest dictionary entirely about music was:

0049　**Vocabularium musicum.** 11th century. Reprinted: Adrien de la Fage, *Essais de diphtérographie musicale* (Paris: O. Legouix, 1864), I, 404-408. ML55 L2

Gustave Reese suggests (*Music in the Middle Ages*, p.147) that the author of this neglected work may have been Johannes Presbyter. It treats (with brief definitions) only 62 terms, most of them Latin.

About four centuries slipped away before the next known music dictionary appeared; it was:

0050　Tinctoris, Jean. **Terminorum musicae diffinitorium.** Treviso: Gerardus de Lisa, ca.1495. ML108 T5

　　　Duckles 67–224; Duckles 74–310

Covers 291 terms in considerable detail, and is still necessary for research into fifteenth century music. Publication date has most often been given as 1475, but recent scholarship prefers 1495; see essay in Coover (0048), and commentary by Coover in:

　　　Dictionary of Musical Terms. An English translation of *Terminorum musicae diffinitorium* together with the Latin text. Tr. and annot. by Carl Parrish. New York: Free Press of Glencoe, 1963. xi, 108p. ML108 T513

Among translations into other languages, there are those of Friedrich Chrysander (in *Jahrbuch der Musikwissenschaft*, I, 1863; German), Armand Machabey (Paris: Richard-Masse, 1951; French), and Lionello Cammarota (Roma: V. Bonacci, 1965; Italian).

Well over a century passed before a successor to Tinctoris appeared in print. It was the work usually identified as the first music dictionary in German:

0051　Praetorius, Michael. **Syntagma musicum** ... Wolffenbüttel: E. Holwein, 1615-20. 3v. in 1. ML100 A2 P8

This is a deep well of early nomenclature on instruments (particularly the organ), notation, form, composition, and performance. See description in Gustave Reese, *Fourscore Classics* (0223) and Coover (0048). Volume I, in Latin, is not too useful. The other volumes are in German.

During the seventeenth century a number of theoretical treatises carried appendices of terms; Coover gives details on fifteen such sources.

General dictionaries of the period should also be considered, as many (96 in Coover) embrace musical terminology.

While the search for an extremely elusive term might take one into such terra obscura, the mainstream of musical language in this era was pretty well captured by the principal eighteenth century dictionaries. The first of these emerged in 1701: two of them, written by authors ignorant of one another's existence.

0052   Janovka, Tomas Baltazar. **Clavis ad   thesaurum magnae artis musicae** . . . Vetero-Pragae: in Magno Collegio Carolino typis Georgij Labaun, 1701. xx, 324 [i.e., 224] p. ML108 A2 J2
Duckles 67–210; Duckles 74–290

Covers some 200 terms, nearly all of them Latin. Rich in detail and musical examples. A good proportion of the vocabulary is not to be found in more modern dictionaries; e.g., "galizona" is missing from 0001, 0002, 0003, and 0004. Lengthy articles on most notational elements give clear picture of baroque understandings. Text entirely in Latin. (Erroneous pagination noted by James Coover.)

0053   Brossard, Sebastien de. **Dictionaire** [*sic*] **de musique contenant une explication des termes grecs, latins, italiens, & françois** . . . Paris: C. Ballard, 1703. (Facsimile ed.–Amsterdam: Antiqua, 1964). xviii, 380p. ML108 B62
Duckles 67–204; Duckles 74–280

This famous dictionary began as a glossary of terms appended to some motets composed by Brossard (1695), then issued in expanded form as a separate work, *Dictionnaire des terms grecs, latins et italiens* (1701). An informative review of the facsimile edition, by Vincent Duckles, appeared in *Notes*, 24-4 (June 1968), 700-701; it distinguishes among the several versions. While most of the work is occupied with terms, there is a biographical section that will be discussed later in this volume.

English language dictionaries of music begin with an anonymous little book that has been much ignored:

0054   **A Short Explication of Such Foreign Words, As Are Made Use of in Musick Books.** London: J. Brotherton, 1724. 93 [3] p. ML108 A2 S39

Corresponds to the glossary section of a method book named *Rules; or a Short and Compleat Method for Attaining to Play a Thorough Bass upon the Harpsicord or Organ* . . . London: Walsh, 1730[?]. The "foreign words" are in fact Italian. Three sources give different dates for *Rules*: Library of Congress says 1715?; Coover, 1724; Smith and Humphries in their bibliography of the printer Walsh give 1730. The author may have been Dr. Pepusch. About 500 terms.

The first "modern" German dictionary came soon after:

0055   Walther, Johann Gottfried. **Musikalisches Lexikon; Oder, musikalische Bibliothek** . . . Leipzig: W. Deer, 1732. (Faksimile-Nachdruck

hrsg. von Richard Schaal. Kassel: Bärenreiter-Verlag, 1953). 659p. 22 fold.pl.(music). (Documenta musicologica, 1.Reihe: Druckschriften-Faksimiles, 3). ML100 W21 1953
Duckles 67–48; Duckles 74–62

A thorough gathering of terms in German, Greek, Latin, Italian, and French, this lexicon is a landmark effort that is still of great value as a guide to baroque usage. Biographical entries are included, so Walther is also a pioneer musical encyclopedia.

The next significant contribution to musical lexicography was:

0056 Grassineau, James. **A Musical Dictionary; Being a Collection of Terms and Characters . . . Abstracted from the Best Authors in the Greek, Latin, Italian, French, and English Languages.** London: J. Wilcox, 1740. 347p. ML108 A2 B7
Duckles 67–209; Duckles 74–289

While this work is usually identified as an expanded translation of Brossard (0053), Coover has shown that it bears at least an equal debt to *Short Explication* (0054). Well illustrated with charts and musical examples. No biographical entries.

Passing over a couple dozen lesser items of the next 28 years, we come to another monument, by a musician better known as a philosopher.

0057 Rousseau, Jean Jacques. **Dictionnaire de musique.** Paris: Veuve Duchesne, 1768. xii, 547p. 13 leaves of music. (Reprint—Hildesheim: Georg Olms; New York: Johnson Reprint Corp., 1969). ML108 R8 1768a
Duckles 67–217; Duckles 74–298; ARBA 71–1234

A very popular book indeed, as demonstrated by the numerous translations and printings (cited in Coover 0048 and RISM 0419). Needed to trace archaic words, especially in French. For example, "ventre," which a modern French dictionary defines only in non-musical contexts, and which does not appear at all in more recent lexica of music, had an acoustical meaning as the nodal point of a vibrating string. Other expressions are often given more detailed treatment here than in later dictionaries.

The works referred to thus far present an extended introduction to the language of music. To probe any farther into terminology will lead us from generality into the various fields of research specialization; to look for more exhaustive analyses of individual terms will force us into musicological considerations. So this appears to be a good cadential point, and a suitable moment to modulate into another group of information sources.

CHAPTER 2

DIRECT INFORMATION SOURCES

These are compendia of facts, biography, history, and pictures which span the musical skies. Most are recent—even "in progress"—but many are from the nineteenth century and one is nearly 200 years old. They have been selected from hundreds of similar works on the basis of unique content or particularly convenient mode of presentation. Included are a number of non-musical sources that do carry certain types of musical information not available elsewhere.

MOST USEFUL ENCYCLOPEDIC WORKS

0058   **Die Musik in Geschichte und Gegenwart; allgemeine Enzyklopädie der Musik** . . . Hrsg. von Friedrich Blume. Kassel: Bärenreiter-Verlag, 1949– (in progress). ML100 M92
Duckles 67–6; Duckles 74–38
Newest, biggest, and best of the multivolume encyclopedias, MGG (as it is usually called) is complete through the 14 alphabetical volumes; still to be published are a supplementary volume and an index. An international group of leading scholars have put together this outstanding resource. There are about 9,000 articles, all in German, with some 7,100 illustrations, of which perhaps a fourth are plates. Strongest features: lists of compositions for composers (generally comprehensive, but sometimes selective: "Ausw.") and books for authors; lists of writings about persons, places and topics; full documentation and scholarly tone throughout. Articles run to grand dimensions for major topics, e.g., Mozart, 138 pages; Liturgische Dramen, 40 pages. Facts are often presented in tabular, chronological, or other useful array. Heavy use of abbreviations—explained in each volume—and the very tight printing style are obstacles to convenient use. Each volume carries a list of plates, of articles in page order, and of contributors with their contributions. There is no subject indexing of any sort in the first 14 volumes. Several noteworthy articles are cited in this handbook under various topics.
Anyone consulting MGG should bear in mind the long time-span of its publication, and the consequent variance in dates for articles at different points in the alphabet.

0059   Grove, Sir George. **Dictionary of Music and Musicians.** 5th ed., ed. by Eric Blom. New York: St. Martin's Press, 1955 (c1954). 9v. 8,923p. Supplementary volume . . . , 1961. xxxii, 493p. (Paperback reprint—St. Martin's, 1970). ML100 G8863 1955
Duckles 67–22; Duckles 74–21

Usually cited as "Grove's Dictionary," this is the only rival to MGG in terms of scope. Coverage is uneven internationally, with Britain in a prominent place, America poorly treated, and Western Europe somewhere between. Many long articles, lists of works for composers (easier to use than MGG for this), some handy arrangements of data—these are good features. But they cannot outweigh the defects of Grove's. Among these defects are a poor sense of balance, which allows too much space to certain entries and too little to more important ones; a reliance on material from earlier editions; weak, very weak, bibliographies; lack of an index; and a paucity of illustrations. Most contributors were British.

The publishing history of Grove's from 1879 appears in 0048. A sixth edition is now in preparation.

0060   **Algemene muziekencyclopedie.** Onder leiding van A. Corbet en Wouter Paap. Antwerpen: Zuid-Nederlandse Uitg., 1957-63. 6v. Aanvullend deel [Supplement]. Ed. Jozef Robijns. Gent-Louvain: Wetenschappelijke Uitgeverij E. Story-Scientia, 1972. 555p. ML100 A4

Duckles 67—2; Duckles 74—2

A fine, universal work that touches most aspects of music: biography, history, non-western topics, jazz, and pop. Articles appear in Dutch, though written and signed by contributors from various countries. A special value attaches to the "synoptic tables" which unfold music history in 54 pages of multi-columnar chronologies. Lists of works; some portraits. No index.

0061   **Encyclopédie de la musique et dictionnaire du Conservatoire** . . . Ed. Albert Lavignac et Lionel de la Laurencie. Paris: C. Delagrave, 1913-31. 11v. ML100 E5

Duckles 67—18; Duckles 74—17

Old as it is, the Lavignac encyclopedia remains a treasury of useful studies. Articles of comprehensive scope were written by specialists and liberally illustrated with drawings. The most valuable section is Part I: a collection of essays on national music (e.g., Jules Rouanet on Arab music, pp. 2676-2944); many of these will be cited in Volume 2 of the present work. Part II, on theory, features a major contribution by Charles Koechlin on the development of harmony after Bizet.

Lack of a thorough index has obstructed full access to this work. There is, however, a partial index by Robert Bruce, in *Notes*, series 1 (May 1936); an offprint is found in many libraries shelved next to the *Encyclopédie*.

0062   Moser, Hans Joachim. **Musik Lexikon.** 4., starkerweiterte Aufl. Hamburg: H. Sikorski, 1955. (1st ed. 1932-35). 2v. viii, 1482p. Ergänzungsband, A-Z., 1963. viii, 287p. ML100 M835 1955

Duckles 67—31; Duckles 74—35

The standard brief handbook in German, known for scholarly summaries on historical topics. Biographical entries include lists of works (not comprehensive) for composers, of books for authors. Token bibliographies follow most articles. Some musical examples; no other illustrations. No index.

0063   Riemann, Hugo. **Riemann Musik Lexikon**. 12. Völlig neubearb. Aufl. hrsg. von Wilibald Gurlitt. Mainz: B. Schott's Söhne; New York: Schott Music Corp., 1959-67. (1st ed. 1882). 3v. ML100 R52 1959
        Duckles 67–38; Duckles 74–46

Almost a century old, Riemann is probably the most widely known and cited musical reference work. The colorful individualism of the original compiler has been muted over its complex publishing history (cf. 0048, #1231-1254), and the format has been adjusted to group biographies in the first two volumes and topics in the third. A German slant is still present.

The Sachteil, vol. 3, was edited by Hans Eggebrecht (Gurlitt died in 1963), an authority on terminology (cf. 0047). Terms and topics are approached through penetrating scholarship, with full documentation.

About 80 authors, most of them German, contributed articles. The great strength of the entire work remains in the area of historical musicology—for which it serves as an ideal vade mecum. Each article is provided with thorough bibliographic references. A particularly valuable contribution is the entry "Quellen," in which principal manuscripts and other sources are carefully described and discussed. Illustrations and musical examples are found throughout. No index.

Riemann has been translated into several languages; Coover notes editions in French, Russian, English, and Norwegian. These are the two best-known translations:

> **Dictionnaire de musique**. Traduit par Georges Humbert. 3.éd. Paris: Payot, 1931. (1st publ. 1902, based on 4th ed. of Riemann). [vii], xv, 1485p. ML100 R59 1931
> Includes additional material on non-German topics.

> **Dictionary of Music**. Translated by J. S. Shedlock. London: Augener, Ltd., 1908. (1st publ. 1893; based on Riemann 4th ed.). 2v. 1908p. (Reprint—New York: Da Capo Press, 1970). (Da Capo Press Music Reprint Series). ML100 R54 1970
>   ARBA 72-1099
> Includes additions by the translator.

0064   Scholes, Percy Alfred. **The Oxford Companion to Music** . . . Ed. by John Owen Ward. 10th ed. London, New York: Oxford University Press, 1970. (1st ed. 1938). ix, 1189p. ML100 S37 1970
        Duckles 67–42; Duckles 74–52; ARBA 71-1236

Before his death in 1958, Percy Scholes had prepared nine editions of this splendid, highly personal dictionary. Under its new editor, the Companion has begun the inevitable move toward balance and objectivity, with the resulting excision of certain Scholesian gems—but most of the work retains the stylish sparkle that made it delightful and unique. While most of the fun comes from definitions in the manner of Ambrose Bierce (e.g., applause: "the custom of showing one's pleasure at beautiful music by immediately following it with an ugly noise . . .''), there are also indescribable effects in many biographical pieces, secured largely through well-placed asides (e.g., of Thomas DuPuis, the last line: "Haydn, meeting him as he was leaving the Chapel Royal, publicly kissed him in appreciation of his extemporaneous fugues"). A more sober value stems from the numerous articles which cumulate facts under unlikely headings, such as Misattributed Compositions, Bird Music, Colour and Music, or Whistling—in which we learn of "an undergraduate" who could "give a fairly reasonable rendering of the Elijah trio 'Lift thine eyes' all by himself."

There are more than 1,000 illustrations, and there is a pronouncing glossary of 7,000 names and terms.

On the negative side, the Companion is not really up to date, despite the addition of 93 new articles and considerable patching in the current edition. Nor is it indexed, nor well documented.

0065   Thompson, Oscar. **The International Cyclopedia of Music and Musicians**. 9th ed. edited by Robert Sain. New York: Dodd, Mead, 1964. (1st ed. 1939). 2476p. ML100 T47
      Duckles 67–45; Duckles 74–58

A thorough gathering of topical and biographical information by authoritative contributors. An American emphasis serves as a useful counterbalance to the British viewpoints found in Grove's and Scholes. Good listings of works for composers, with chronological summaries on most people. Though revision has been unsteady through the nine editions, contemporary musicians are well represented. There is a pronouncing glossary. Weaknesses are lack of an index and of bibliographical references. Illustrations are scarce.

OTHER WORKS OF ENCYCLOPEDIC SCOPE

0066   Champlin, John Denison. **Cyclopedia of Music and Musicians** . . . New York: C. Scribner's Sons, 1888-90. 3v. 472, 611, 624p. ML100 C45

Later printings in 1893, 1899, and 1903 are shown by the National Union Catalog. An uneven work which does have use for its 1,217 portraits of musicians, autograph signatures, facsimiles, and other illustrations. Biographical articles predominate: many are of persons omitted from later sources; some have bibliographic references to Fétis (0191 below), Mendel (0079), etc. There are also entries under names of compositions, including individual arias from operas—many of these works are quite obscure today.

0067   **A Dictionary of Modern Music and Musicians**. General editor: A. Eaglefield Hull. London: Dent; New York: Dutton, 1924. xvi, 543p. (Reprint—New York: Da Capo Press, 1971; St. Clair Shores, Mich.: Scholarly Press, 1972). (Da Capo Press Music Reprint Series). ML100 D5
      Duckles 67–53; Duckles 74–72; ARBA 72–1094; ARBA 73–1026

A major handbook on the period from about 1880, strong in

biography, with good coverage of technical topics, organizations, festivals, and music of various countries. Written by 115 international contributors. Bibliographies and lists of works are very fine.

0068   Dunstan, Ralph. **A Cyclopaedic Dictionary of Music.** 4th ed. London: J. Curwen & Sons; Philadelphia: Curwen, Inc., 1925. (1st ed. 1908). ix, 632p. (Reprint: New York: Da Capo Press, 1973). (Da Capo Press Music Reprint Series). ML100 D92 1925
        Duckles 67−15; Duckles 74−14; ARBA 74−1075
A curious collection of facts, such as musical "firsts" (e.g., first use of three staves in pianoforte writing, by Pollini), quotations and attributions ("Father of the German Lied" was H. Albert), birthdays of musicians. Worth remembering for its probably unique table of bird music—with ratings of various birds according to mellowness, compass, execution and sprightliness. Documentation lacking throughout; reliability open to question; still, this is a work of occasional value.

0069   **Enciclopedia della musica.** Direttore: Claudio Sartori. Milano: Ricordi, 1963-64. 4v. 584, 596, 574, 628p. ML100 E45
        Duckles 67−16; Duckles 74−16
Forms, terms, biographies; good illustrations, some in color. Written by some 230 specialists from many countries—but individual articles are unsigned, for the most part. Emphasis is on recent music and personalities. Bibliographies are provided, but they must be faulted for important omissions. No index.

0070   **Encyclopaedia Britannica.** Chicago: Encyclopaedia Britannica. (1st ed. 1768-71). 24v. AE5 E363
        Winchell 67−AD2; ARBA 71−171
Winchell gives a concise publishing history of this very important work, which is now issued annually on a "continuous revision" basis. Music editor for the 1973 printing was the noted scholar Gerald Abraham; with the equally celebrated Nicholas Slonimsky identified as editor for American music. Among the expert contributors were Anthony Baines (on instruments), Margaret Dean-Smith (on folk music), Edward Lockspeiser (on French music), and Donald Francis Tovey. (Tovey was music editor of EB during its "golden age"; he was a brilliant commentator whose numerous articles in the encyclopedia became classics—but only parts of a few essays by him remain in the new printing.) In general the quality of the music articles is good, but EB does not seem to seek out the very best authorities for individual topics ... with a few exceptions such as those already cited. Undoubtedly the key information function of the set lies in the fact of its annual revision: there is a good chance of very recent data appearing. But this is not invariable: e.g., the article (1972) on Leonard Bernstein cites no composition later than 1965; yet it does mention his retirement from the New York Philharmonic in 1969. The article on Pierre Boulez (1972) cites no composition later than 1965, nor does it allude to his appointment as Bernstein's successor with the Philharmonic. A major feature of Britannica is

its very thorough index of more than 400,000 entries; ease of access is immeasurably simpler here than in any musical encyclopedia.

0071   **Encyclopedia Americana.** New York: Americana Corp. (1st ed. 1829-33). 30v. AE5 E333
         Winchell 67—AD1; ARBA 71—170
There are no musicians among the "advisory editors" identified in the 1973 printing (EA is also a "continuous revision" work), which may account for the uneven quality of musical articles. Some outstanding scholars are among the authors: Gilbert Chase, Karl Geiringer, Bruno Nettl, Gustave Reese, and Nicholas Slonimsky, for instance; but balance and coordination are lacking. Not up to date, either: the Leonard Bernstein article (1973) cites no work beyond 1963; the one on Boulez takes him only to 1956. The index is excellent.

0072   **Encyclopédie de la musique.** Publié sous la direction de François Michel en collaboration avec François Lesure et Vladimir Féderov . . . Paris: Fasquelle, 1958-61. 3v. ML100 E48
         Duckles 67—17; Duckles 74—16
The first volume begins with a "Livre d'or": facsimiles of scores, autographs, portraits and comments from various modern composers. A useful survey of music festivals, by country; sections on the French concert scene, European radio, the teaching of music in France, music publication, French copyright law, institutions. A 31-page chronology presents highlights in history of ideas, art, and literature as well as music, up to 1951, with dates of major compositions shown. Main text includes terms, biographies, topics; these are uneven in coverage and documentation—best treatment is of contemporary music. Illustrations mostly of poor quality. There is a valuable article on musical ethnography. No index.

0073   **Encyclopédie méthodique, ou par ordre de matières . . .: "Musique."** Compiled by Nicolas Étienne Framery, *et al.* Paris: Panckoucke, 1791-1818. 2v. (Reprint—New York: Da Capo Press, 1971). (Da Capo Press Music Reprint Series). ML100 A2 F8
         Duckles 67—19; Duckles 74—18
These two volumes on music were part of a large general encyclopedia. The basis for them was the corpus of writing on music which Jean Jacques Rousseau had published in his *Dictionnaire de musique* (0057) and in the Diderot Encyclopedia, with later revisions. Terms, organization, topical articles; no biographies or illustrations; no index.

0074   **Encyclopedie van de muziek.** Hoofdredactie: L. M. G. Arntzenius *et al.* Amsterdam: Elsevier, 1956-57. 2v. ML100 E55
         Duckles 67—20; Duckles 74—19
A good general work with universal coverage of topics and persons, strongest for the Low Countries. Valuable chronological graph (pp. 30-47), with horizontal orientation by country and color coding for types of music. Some photographs which would be hard to find elsewhere—e.g., one of the Hotcha Trio, a Dutch group, shown playing their harmonicas. No index.

0075   Koch, Willi August. **Musisches Lexikon: Künstler, Kunstwerke und Motive aus Dichtung, Musik und bildender Kunst.** 2., veränderte und erweiterte Aufl. Stuttgart: A. Kröner, 1964. (1st ed. 1956). 1250 cols., xxxx p. N31 K57

An interesting, uneven endeavor to blend the visual and literary arts with music. Separate articles on people and topics from each field, with some cross-coverage (e.g., reference in the D'Annunzio article to Debussy's setting of the Martyrdom of St. Sebastian; similar allusions in many entries for authors). The idea is not carried out fully, however. Limited to European culture. A strong index, which includes titles of works mentioned (but one must look for most of them in their German versions). Illustrated with 876 photos and four color plates.

0076   LaBorde, Jean Benjamin de. **Essai sur la musique ancienne et moderne.** Paris: P. D. Pierres, 1780. 4v.

Duckles 67−347; Duckles 74−430

A very important compilation of detailed information on several topics; valuable for the facts presented and also for the perspective it offers on musical scholarship in pre-revolutionary France. Highlights of the four volumes: I.−geographical survey of music in antiquity, featuring an elaborate foldout on Greek notation and a lavishly detailed, beautifully illustrated essay on Chinese music; also studies of instruments used by various peoples and for certain occasions; sections on modern music in Russia, Greece, Siam, etc. II.−thorough history of song in antiquity and in France, with texts given, biographical notes on the poets, much actual music printed, some in four-part settings. III.−biographical dictionary of Greek and Roman poets and musicians (132p.); a list of classical writers who mentioned music, with the allusions cited (27p.); biographical dictionary for Italians, with another list of those who have mentioned music (164p.); similar treatment of Frenchmen. IV.−more French lyric poets, and a wondrous index to all personal names in the four volumes as well as subjects.

0077   **Larousse de la musique.** Publié sous la direction de Norbert Dufourcq . . . Paris: Larousse, 1957. 2v. 626, 644p. ML100 L28

Duckles 67−27; Duckles 74−30

By some 120 (mostly French) contributors. Terms, topics, biographies, titles of pieces. Good photos on slick paper; good maps; good separate bibliographical section. But information is not always reliable, and very frequently out of date.

0078   **Larousse Encyclopedia of Music** . . . Ed., Geoffrey Hindley . . . 1st American ed. New York: World Publishing Co., 1971. 576p. ML160 L34

Duckles 74−492; ARBA 72−1098

Based on Norbert Dufourcq's *La Musique, les hommes, les instruments, les oeuvres* (Paris: Larousse, 1965). Topical articles, in large affinity groups. Terms in a separate glossary. Some useful survey material, with excellent illustrations, many in color. Contributors not identified; no documentation given. Folk music particularly well covered. Good index of titles, persons, and topics.

0079   Mendel, Hermann. **Musikalisches Conversations-Lexikon: Eine Ency-
        klopädie der gesammten musikalischen Wissenschaften** . . . 3. Ausg.
        Leipzig: List & Francke, 1890-91. (1st ed. 1870-79). 11v. ML100
        M53
        Duckles 67—28; Duckles 74—32
An interesting picture of musical life and knowledge a hundred years
ago, but also valuable for biographical entries on obscure people and for a
number of lengthy survey articles. Worth noting are the studies of "Akustik"
(47p.), "Literatur" (a 49-page bibliographic essay that cites articles and books
and includes a list of libraries in major European cities), and individual
countries (e.g., 58 pages on the music of Portugal). Awkward to use, since
there is no general index; but each volume has a "Verzeichnis," which is
really a handy alphabetical list of its articles. Various editors and authors gave
their assistance.

0080   Moore, John Weeks. **Complete Encyclopedia of Music** . . . Boston:
        J. P. Jewett and Co.; New York: Sheldon, Lamport and Blakeman,
        1854. Appendix. Boston: O. Ditson; New York: C. H. Ditson Co.,
        c1875. 45p.
        Duckles 67—30; Duckles 74—34
The base volume was reissued by O. Ditson in 1880 with the
Appendix bound in. Terms, topical articles and biographies, largely adapted
from European predecessors. The style is reminiscent of that in the Oxford
Companion (0064): personal views are blended liberally with facts. Various
unusual subjects are taken up—e.g., "Influence of Music on Animals"—but the
prime utility of the work is for facts on long-forgotten musicians (where else
can we find 2½ pages about the early nineteenth century composer John
Bernhard Logier?). Unfortunately, there are no entries for titles of compositions, nor lists of works under names of composers; nor is there a general
index.

0081   **La Musica: Enciclopedia storica**. Sotto la direzione di Guido M.
        Gatti. A cura di Alberto Basso. Torino: Unione Tipografico-Editrice
        Torinese, 1966. Part I: 4v. Part II: in progress. ML100 M93
        Duckles 74—36; Winchell 67—2BH17; 3BH14
In the first four volumes there are 196 long articles (81 of them
biographical) illustrated by 30 plates and 1,400 black and white photos.
Many contributors—all but four of them European. Lists of works under
composers' names. Good surveys of music by country. Part II is a biographcal
and topical dictionary of shorter entries; it includes some indexes that cover
the main set as well.

0082   **Musikens hven-hvad-hvor**. Udarbejdet af Nelly Backhausen og Axel
        Kjerulf. København: Politikens Forlag, 1950. 3v. ML102 M9 M9
        Duckles 67—72; Duckles 74—94
Volume I is a discursive chronology of music history, with extended
commentaries on persons as they occur; it has a good index. In the other two
volumes we find a strong collection of biographical sketches: international
(though best for Scandinavians) and inclusive of jazz and pop musicians as

well as serious artists. Many portraits. Volume III also contains a remarkable title listing of some 15,000 serious and popular works, mostly given in their original languages, with composers and dates. Few other sources will reveal that it was Pete Wending who penned "Yacka Hula Hickey Dula," back in 1916.

0083   Pena, Joaquin. **Diccionario de la música Labor.** Iniciado por Joaquin Pena, continuado por Higinio Anglés, con la colaboración de Miguel Querol . . . Barcelona: Labor, 1954. 2v. x, 2318p. ML105 P4
       Duckles 67–36; Duckles 74–42

Biographical and topical articles by Spanish and Latin American contributors. Despite the 1954 publication date, effective cutoff date seems to have been in the early 1940s (when work on the dictionary began). For example, the fine survey of music libraries by country, with holdings and bibliographic references (pp. 263-88), was written in 1941. Some other interesting articles are "Asociaciones Musicales," an international survey; "Barcelona"; and "Canción Popular Española." Classified lists of works appear in composer biographies.

0084   Pratt, Waldo S. **The New Encyclopedia of Music and Musicians.** New and rev. ed. New York: Macmillan, 1929. (1st ed. 1924). 969p. ML100 P87
       Duckles 67–37; Duckles 74–43

Terms, biographies, topics, concentrating on the eighteenth to the twentieth centuries and on American matters. Useful lists of works for minor composers. A special feature is the musical gazetteer (pp. 901-960), which shows what music events, organizations, sources, libraries, and individuals have been associated with various cities.

0085   Sacher, Jack. **Music A to Z.** Based on the work of Rudolf Stephan. Translators: Mieczyslaw Kolinski, *et al.* New York: Grosset & Dunlap, c1963. viii, 432p. (Universal Reference Library). ML100 S82 1963
       Duckles 67–218; Duckles 74–299

The Stephan work was *Musik* (Frankfurt: Fischer, 1957). This version has been expanded to give more coverage to English, American, French, and Italian music; e.g., in articles "Song," "Symphony," "Opera," and "Oratorio." Some new articles also, notably one on jazz by Bert Konowitz. Long articles on many topics; an appendix of terms; and a strong general index which includes names of compositions cited in the main text.

0086   Sandved, Kjell Bloch. **Musikkens verden; familiens musikkbok.** Oslo: Musikkens Verden Forlag, 1951, c1950. 2238 cols. ML100 S246 1951a
       Duckles 74–48

A "coffee-table" book of biography and musical topics treated in very general terms. Personal opinion mingled with facts. Most useful for its 2,000 photographs, which run from Bach's organ in Arnstadt to the Andrews Sisters and a topless view of Josephine Baker. Sandved has been widely translated, with each version adding and subtracting material in accord with its national interests. The English manifestation—minus the Baker topless— appeared in London (and later New York with some American emphasis) under the name *World of Music*. Unindexed, uneven, but occasionally useful.

0087   Schilling, Gustav. **Encyclopädie der gesamten musikalischen Wissen-schaften** . . . Stuttgart: F. H. Köhler, 1835-38. 6v. Supplement-Band, 1842. ML100 S33
        Duckles 67—40; Duckles 74—49
This large, important work includes terms, names, and topics in one alphabet. Articles vary from brief notices to long essays (e.g., Akustik, 19p.), but most are a page or two for major subjects. Not illustrated, except for examples in musical notation. No index. Useful today for details on persons, especially German, not found in modern compilations; and, of course, for the cross-section view it permits us of musical knowledge at a time when musicology was in its infancy.

0088   Seeger, Horst. **Musik Lexikon**. Leipzig: Deutscher Verlag für Musik, 1966. 2v. ML100 S415
        Duckles 74—54
Biographies (international, serious, and popular artists), topics and titles of compositions all in one alphabet. Up-to-date information on persons and organizations—e.g., orchestras and opera companies. Bibliographic refer-ences are weak, and there is no index. Lists of works for composers; of books for authors.

0089   **The World Book Encyclopedia**. Chicago: Field Enterprises Educa-tional Corp. (1st ed. 1917). 22v. AE5 W55
        ARBA 72—196 (for 1972 ed.)
With all factors considered, this may well be the world's finest encyclopedia. Although intended for young readers, it serves non-specialized needs of adults also. Revised annually, it provides the most current data available in any general encyclopedia. It must be added that music coverage is rather uneven—judged by the high standard of the work as a whole. Music consultant is Professor James A. Sykes of Dartmouth; some important scholars have assisted him (e.g., Karl Geiringer, Claude Palisca, Homer Ulrich), but some articles seem to have been written by less qualified persons. Referring to the Leonard Bernstein article (cf. comments under 0070 and 0071), we find mention of his celebrated work of 1971, the Mass. Under Boulez, we find reference to his appointment as music director of the New York Philharmonic in 1971; however, the latest composition credited to him dates from 1957. The index volume is a treasury: it presents titles of musical works, from folk songs to tone poems, and names of musical personalities from all times and places. Portraits and other illustrations are more numerous in WB than in any other work of its kind: altogether there are some 29,000, with 10,000 in color.

0090 **Zenei lexicon.** Írták Szabolcsi Bence és Tóth Aladár. Átdolgozott új kiadás, főszerkesztő: Bartha Dénes; szerkesztő: Tóth Margit. Budapest: Zeneműkiadó, 1965— . 3v. 683, 726, 768p. ML100 Z43
Duckles 67–50; Duckles 74–64
A strong compilation of terms, titles, topics, and biographical entries. Coverage is international, though not without Hungarian emphasis. Works (or books) are listed in personal entries. Popular musicians as well as serious artists are included. About 70 contributors have initialed the articles; most of them are Hungarian. Few illustrations; no index.

Another encyclopedic work, by Torrellas, has been cited (0008) among the term dictionaries; it covers—in volumes 2, 3, and 4—biographical and historical topics, and lists many works by title.
Topical articles are also found in Apel's *Harvard Dictionary* (0002), and in Panum (0021).
There are many important general encyclopedias in addition to the three cited above. While *Britannica, Americana*, and *World Book* appear to be the most valuable for musical inquiries, the reader may also turn profitably to *Collier's Encyclopedia* (USA), *Brockhaus Enzyklopädie* (BRD; new ed. 1966—), *Meyers enzyklopädisches Lexikon in 25 Bänden* (BRD, 1971—), *Grote Winkler Prins* (Netherlands, new ed. 1966—), *Svensk Uppslagsbok* (Sweden, 1957-63), and *Diccionario enciclopedico Salvat universal* (Spain, 1969—)—to mention only some recent issues. Even older sets, like the *Enciclopedia italiana*, may yield musical information, but in general such data will also be present in newer or more specialized works. Winchell and ARBA are excellent guides to publication in this genre.
To conclude this section on dictionaries and encyclopedias, it must be emphasized that no attempt has been made to be comprehensive; indeed, hundreds of likely titles were considered for inclusion, but omitted on the grounds of overlapping with other works of *relative* lack of information value compared with the works included. Thus, quite respectable efforts like the Jack Westrup *New College Encyclopedia of Music* are omitted simply because they do not add to the range of facts that can be drawn from the more substantial sources assembled here.

PRINCIPAL HISTORIES

Most of the titles that follow are large reference histories on a universal scale, whether in single volumes or in series. Historical writing that is specialized by topic or region will be found listed in volumes II and III of the present work.

0091 Abbiati, Franco. **Storia della musica.** 2d ed. Milano: Garzanti, 1943-46. 5v. ML160 A224
Duckles 67–291; Duckles 74–376
A very well illustrated history, arranged by period and country. Good summary of modern Italian music (IV, 521-86). Excerpts from other

books included in each chapter; bibliographies at the end. Footnotes generally lacking. The index is not expansive.

0092   Adler, Guido. **Handbuch der Musikgeschichte** ... 2. vollständig ... Aufl. Berlin: H. Keller, 1930. (1st ed. 1924). 2v. (Reprint–Tutzing: Schneider, 1961). ML160 A3
        Duckles 67–292; Duckles 74–377
A learned, analytical approach in chrono-topical format. Bibliographies after each chapter, but no footnotes. Many expert contributors: Curt Sachs, Peter Wagner, Egon Wellesz, etc. Index to names only. The principal gathering of facts and views from the most brilliant era of German musicology, but otherwise not of great practical value today.

0093   Ambros, August Wilhelm. **Geschichte der Musik** ... 3. gänzlich umgearb. Aufl. Leipzig: Leuckart, 1887-1911. (1st ed. 1862-81). 5v. (Reprint–Hildesheim: Georg Olms, 1968). ML160 A493
        Duckles 67–293; Duckles 74–378
An outstanding one-man history, completed and revised after Ambros' death by a number of other scholars. Most valuable for the medieval and renaissance periods, which Ambros had researched carefully; the approach is scholarly throughout: detail, footnotes, name and topical indexes. Volume 5 is made up of musical examples from the fifteenth and sixteenth centuries. A great deal of material here that has not appeared in later histories.

0094   Bernard, Robert. **Histoire de la musique.** Paris: Nathan, 1961-71. 5v. ML160 B563
        Duckles 67–294; Duckles 74–379
The most lavish of recent histories, beautifully illustrated and elegantly produced. Nothing very spectacular about the content, however, which is generally acceptable but often distorted; cf. the sundry misguidance offered in the section on American musicology, which even cites that old bibliographic "ghost," Lang's *Music in the Classic Era* (announced but never published). Little documentation. A title, composer, and subject index is found in the final volume.

0095   Bücken, Ernst. **Handbuch der Musikwissenschaft.** Wildpark-Potsdam: Akademische Verlagsgesellschaft Athenaion, 1928-34. 13v. (Reprint–New York: Musurgia, 1949; 13v. in 9). ML160 B9 B89
        Duckles 67–297; Duckles 74–381-394
Consists of the following independent monographs:

Besseler, Heinrich. **Die Musik des Mittelalters und der Renaissance.** 337p.

#Blume, Friedrich. **Die evangelische Kirchenmusik.** 171p. (Later issued as *Geschichte der evangelischen Kirchenmusik.* Hrsg. Ludwig Finscher *et al.*, Kassel: Bärenreiter, 1965, 465p.).

Bücken, Ernst. **Geist und Form im musikalischen Kunstwerk.** 195p.

Bücken, Ernst. **Die Musik des 19. Jahrhunderts bis zur Moderne.** 319p.

Bücken, Ernst. **Die Musik des Rokokos und der Klassik.** 247p.

#Haas, Robert. **Aufführungspraxis der Musik.** 298p.

Haas, Robert. **Die Musik des Barocks.** 290p.

Heinitz, Wilhelm. **Instrumentenkunde.** 159p.

Lachmann, Robert. **Die Musik der aussereuropäischen Natur- und Kulturvölker.** 33p.

Sachs, Curt. **Die Musik der Antike.** 32p.

#Panóff, Peter. **Die altslavische Volks- und Kirchenmusik.** 31p.

Mersmann, Hans. **Die moderne Musik seit der Romantik.** 225p.

#Ursprung, Otto. **Die katholische Kirchenmusik.** 312p.

The sign # preceding certain titles indicates that they will be referred to again later in the present work. A well-organized, scholarly series, much of it still useful. Excellent illustrations; but the color plates of the original issue were not carried in the Musurgia reprint.

0096   Burney, Charles. **A General History of Music, from the Earliest Times to the Present Period.** London: Printed for the Author, 1776-89. 4v. (Reprint—Ed. Frank Mercer. London: Foulis; New York: Harcourt, 1935. 4v. in 2. Reprint of Mercer ed.—New York: Dover Publications, 1957. 2v.). ML159 B96
        Duckles 67—311; Duckles 74—395
Along with Hawkins' history (0098) of the same year, this is considered to mark the onset of modern musical historical writing. Most valued today for its first-hand view of eighteenth century music, and for its polished style.

0097   Grout, Donald Jay. **A History of Western Music.** Rev. ed. New York: Norton, 1973. (1st ed. 1960). ML160 G87
        Duckles 67—325 (for 1st ed.); Duckles 74—408; Winchell 67—BY75 (for 1st ed.)
This is the standard one-volume coverage of the musical past in the English language, directed to college students or general readers. Many illustrations and musical examples; annotated bibliography.

0098   Hawkins, Sir John. **A General History of the Science and Practice of Music.** London: Payne and Son, 1776. 5v. Reissued, with help of Hawkins' posthumous notes, London: Novello, 1853; this edition reprinted by Novello, 1875. (Reprint of Novello 1853, with introduction by Charles Cudworth—New York: Dover, 1963. 2v.). ML159 H39
        Duckles 67—329; Duckles 74—412

While Hawkins' style and musical insights are regarded as inferior to those of his contemporary rival, Burney (0096), his history is still quite useful. It includes extensive translations into English of early treatises, and complete musical compositions printed as examples. One volume is made up of portraits.

0099 Kretzschmar, Hermann. **Kleine Handbücher der Musikgeschichte nach Gattungen.** Leipzig: Breitkopf & Härtel, 1905-22. 14v. in 15.
Duckles 67—332-346; Duckles 74—415-429
Consists of the following monographs:

Schering, Arnold. **Geschichte des Instrumentalkonzerts.** 226p.

#Leichtentritt, Hugo. **Geschichte der Motette.** 453p.

Kretzschmar, Hermann. **Geschichte des neuen deutsches Liedes.** 354p.

Schmitz, Eugen. **Geschichte der Kantate und des geistlichen Konzerts.** 327p.

Kretzschmar, Hermann. **Geschichte der Oper.** 286p.

Kretzschmar, Hermann. **Einführung in die Musikgeschichte.** 82p.

#Wolf, Johannes. **Handbuch der Notationskunde.** 2v.

Botsiber, Hugo. **Geschichte der Ouvertüre und der freien Orchesterformen.** 274p.

#Schünemann, Georg. **Geschichte des Dirigierens.** 359p.

#Wagner, Peter. **Geschichte der Messe.** 548p.

#Sachs, Curt. **Handbuch der Musikinstrumentenkunde.** 412p.

#Aber, Adolf. **Handbuch der Musikliteratur** . . . 696 cols.

Nef, Karl. **Geschichte der Symphonie und Suite.** 344p.

Titles labelled with the # will be treated more fully at later points in the present work. The other titles have been more or less superseded by recent research.

0100 Lang, Paul Henry. **Music in Western Civilization.** New York: Norton, 1941. 1107p. ML160 L25 M8
Duckles 67—348; Duckles 74—431
A major contribution, endeavoring to show connections between music history and developments in other spheres of activity.

0101 **New Oxford History of Music.** Ed. Jack A. Westrup, *et al.* London: Oxford University Press, 1954— (in progress). ML160 N44
Duckles 67—360; Duckles 74—435-439; Winchell 67—BH80; 2BH21
Planned to be 10 volumes. The following have appeared:

Wellesz, Egon. **Ancient and Oriental Music.** 1957. 530p.

Hughes, Dom Anselm. **Early Medieval Music up to 1300**. 1954. 434p.

Hughes, Dom Anselm, and Gerald Abraham. **Ars Nova and the Renaissance**. 1960. 565p.

Abraham, Gerald. **The Age of Humanism, 1540-1630**. 1968. 978p.

These four titles will be given fuller attention in Volume III of the present work. The series is a replacement for an earlier *Oxford History of Music* (2d ed. London: Oxford University Press, 1929-38), which is no longer of use.

0102 **Norton History of Music**. New York: Norton, 1940– (in progress).
      Duckles 67–352-359; Duckles 74–440-446; Winchell 67–BH78
This series title has been imposed by common usage on a group of music histories issued by Norton:

Reese, Gustave. **Music in the Middle Ages**. 1940. 502p.

Sachs, Curt. **The Rise of Music in the Ancient World** . . . 1943. 324p.

Salazar, Alfredo. **Music in Our Time**. 1946. 367p.

Bukofzer, Manfred. **Music in the Baroque Era** . . . 1947. 489p.

Einstein, Alfred. **Music in the Romantic Era**. 1947. 371p.

Reese, Gustave. **Music in the Renaissance**. 1954; rev. ed. 1959. 1002p.

Wiora, Walter. **The Four Ages of Music**. 1965. 233p.

Austin, William. **Music in the 20th Century** . . . 1966. 708p.

All these titles will be taken up at appropriate places in Volume III. It may be said at this point, however, that they clearly constitute the major scholarly overview of music history.

0103 **Prentice-Hall History of Music Series**. Ed. H. Wiley Hitchcock.
      Englewood Cliffs, N.J.: Prentice-Hall, 1965-69. 9v.
      Duckles 67–373; Duckles 74–456-464
      Consists of the following:

Seay, Albert. **Music in the Medieval World**. 1965. 182p. ML172 S4 M9

Newman, Joel. **Renaissance Music**. In preparation.

Palisca, Claude. **Baroque Music**. 1968. 230p. ML193 P34

Pauly, Reinhard G. **Music in the Classic Period**. 1965. 214p. ML196 P38

Longyear, Rey M. **Nineteenth-Century Romanticism in Music**. 1969. 220p. ML196 L65

Salzman, Eric. **Twentieth-Century Music: An Introduction**. 1967. 196p. ML197 S17

Nettl, Bruno. **Folk and Traditional Music of the Western Continents.** 1965. 2d ed. 1973. 213p. ML3549 N5

Malm, William P. **Music Cultures of the Pacific, the Near East, and Asia.** 1967. 169p. ML330 M3

Hitchcock, H. Wiley. **Music in the United States: An Historical Introduction.** 1969. 270p. ML200 H58

This unusual series succeeds in blending a number of typically incompatible elements: erudition, readability, and brevity. Written by leading scholars, these volumes are nevertheless quite suitable for students and "informed laymen." They are well documented and replete with musical examples plus attractive illustrations. Each volume will be given further attention in the third part of the present work.

0104   Strunk, Oliver. **Source Readings in Music History from Classical Antiquity through the Romantic Era.** New York: Norton, 1950. 919p. ML160 S89
    Duckles 67–384; Duckles 74–473

Well-chosen group of 87 writings by musicians and critics, with new English translations where necessary, and perceptive commentaries. Only brief extracts from long treatises are given. Since 1950, when this work appeared, many of the old theorists have been fully translated into English; but Strunk is still a convenient gathering of many highlights from their writings.

CHRONOLOGIES

All chronologies have this much in common: they record events in a year-to-year series. But they vary in what kind of events are recorded—and regarding choice of events within a type—as well as in amount of information provided. And naturally there are differences in time spans covered or emphasized. The group that follows takes in a wide spectrum of possibilities.

0105   Alexander, Franz. **Kleine Musikgeschichte in Jahresübersichten.** Leipzig: Ahrens Nachf. Carl Zierow, 1933. 121p. ML105 A375

Births, deaths, premieres; from 676 B.C. to 1933. Very weak before the nineteenth century, but improves thereafter.

0106   Detheridge, Joseph. **Chronology of Music Composers.** Birmingham: the Author, 1936. 2v. (Reprint—St. Clair Shores, Mich.: Scholarly Press, 1972). Vol. I: 820-1810; xviii, 143p. Vol. II: 1810-1937; viii, 168p. ML161 D35
    Duckles 67–389; Duckles 74–499; ARBA 73–1039

The most extended list of composers in date order: some 2,500 names, from Notker Balbulus (d.912 A.D.) to Benjamin Britten. Columns for birth, death, nationality, and brief identification. Index; fold-out time chart; list of innovators (first cello soloist, first to write orchestral crescendo, etc.); some portraits. Unfortunately, not always reliable in terms of facts and dates.

0107   Documents du demi-siècle: Tableau chronologique des principales oeuvres musicales de 1900 à 1950 ... By Henri Louis de la Grange. Paris: R. Masse, 1952. 146p. "Numéro spécial" de *La Revue Musicale*, No. 216, année 1952. ML5 R613
Duckles 67–620; Duckles 74–808

Annual summary, in three columns by genre, of major works. No information other than titles, and occasionally the instrumentation of certain ensemble pieces. Useful for obscure works, and for the visual immediacy of the format.

0108   Gutknecht, Félicie. **Tabellen zur Musik- und Kulturgeschichte.** Basel, 1962. 48 l. (mimeographed). ML161 G88

Begins in the fourth millenium B.C.; last music entry is 1961. Separate columns for musical and cultural/historical events. Birth and death dates somewhat inconsistently provided. Main value would be for listing of modern compositions (performance dates), especially German and mid-European; not much duplication with 0105, 0106, or 0107.

0109   Lowe, C. Egerton. **A Chronological Cyclopedia of Musicians and Musical Events from A.D. 320 to 1896 ... Biographical Notices of Upwards of 1,000 of the Chief Musicians ... and a Summary of over 700 of the Chief Musical Events of the World ...** London: Weekes & Co., 1896. 126p. ML105 L91

The first section of this ambitious endeavor is a list of musicians arranged by year of birth (pp. 1-86); the second section is a sequence of sundry occurrences such as premieres, openings of opera houses, anniversaries of earlier events, festivals, appearances of great musicians in certain cities, establishment of periodicals, etc. (pp. 87-112). Indexes to both sections. A highly useful compilation, hardly duplicated by the other chronologies cited here.

0110   Mies, Paul, and N. Schneider. **Musik im Umkreis der Kulturgeschichte: Ein Tabellenwerk aus der Geschichte der Musik, Literatur, bildenden Künste, Philosophie und Politik Europas.** Köln: P. J. Tonger, 1953. 2v. ML161 M52
Duckles 67–391; Duckles 74–504

Vol. I: musical events, with comments, in topical lists by date. Vol. II: tabular presentation of general, literary, and artistic history, in columns by country. Remarkably detailed.

0111   Schering, Arnold. **Tabellen zur Musikgeschichte ...** 5. Auflage bis zur Gegenwart ergänzt von Hans Joachim Moser. Wiesbaden: Breitkopf & Härtel, 1962. (1st ed. 1914). 174p. ML161 S273 1962
Duckles 67–392; Duckles 74–505

Reaches from the Sumerians to 1962. Discursive account of events, stylistic developments, personal data, performances, establishment of organizations, publications; these in one sequence, accompanied by columns that cite non-musical happenings. Index to persons, in which works are presented in chronological order under each composer. To emphasize value of consulting more than one chronology, it can be noted that compositions listed for 1941 in Schering are *entirely* different titles from those given by 0107 for that year. And while Schering is much the larger book, Gutknecht (0108) often mentions events not found in Schering.

0112   Slonimsky, Nicolas. **Music since 1900.** 4th ed. New York: Scribner's, 1971. (1st ed. 1937). 1595p. ML197 S634
    Duckles 67–393 (for 3rd ed.); Duckles 74–506; ARBA 72–1084
Covers events through July 20, 1969. A thorough list of premieres and other developments, including popular and Broadway music, with emphasis on Americana; births and deaths also indicated. Excellent indexing. Letters and documents relating to twentieth century music are offered in a separate section.

Other chronologies of importance appear in works cited earlier: 0060, 0072, 0074, and 0082. See also 0119. National and topical chronologies are described in later volumes.

ICONOGRAPHIES

"The art of representation by pictures or images," is one meaning given to iconography by Webster 2. In the present group of works, this definition is interpreted to cover illustrations of actual music (primarily autograph scores), portraits of musicians, musical activity as shown in paintings or photographs, and all sorts of guides and indexes to such material. Other types of illustration—such as facsimiles of music printing, or pictures of musical instruments—have been reserved for Volume III.
Serious interest in musical iconography began with the publication of Kinsky's *Geschichte der Musik in Bildern* in 1930 (0120). But the subject has only recently been accorded systematic attention. In 1971 there was inaugurated within the International Association of Music Libraries a project entitled "Répertoire International d'Iconographie Musicale" (RIdIM); it functions in cooperation with the International Musicological Society and the International Council of Museums. RIdIM—the third major international bibliographic effort of the Association (cf. RILM 0260 and RISM 0419) —aims to optimize access to and use of all visual materials relating to music. An account of plans and initial activities will be found in *Fontes artis musicae*, 19 (Sept.-Dec. 1972/73), 196-206.
The first two items listed below are basic bibliographies that were distributed at the RIdIM session just mentioned:

0113   Crane, Frederick. **The Iconography of Music: An Annotated Bibliography.** Iowa City, the Author. 41p. (mimeographed).
List of catalogs, illustrated histories, and other pictorial studies.

0114   Van de Waal, Hans. **Preliminary List of Iconographic Literature in the Field of Music** . . . Leiden: the Author.

Also discussed at the RIdIM meeting of 1971 was the book—then in press—by Howard Mayer Brown, which presents a system for classifying and indexing the musical elements in art. The system makes possible the classification of paintings and prints in terms of instruments shown, country, subject matter, time period, etc.

0115   Brown, Howard Mayer, and Joan Lascelle. **Musical Iconography: A Manual for Cataloging Musical Subjects in Western Art before 1800** . . . Cambridge: Harvard University Press, 1972. xiii, 220p. ML111 B825 M9
        Duckles 74–1840; ARBA 74–908

We now turn to some major examples of iconographical publication: collections of pictures and indexes to such collections.

0116   Accademia Filarmonica, Bologna. **Catalogo della collezione d'autografi lasciata alla R. Accademia** . . . Bologna: Forni, 1969. xv, 435p. ML135 B6 A3 1969
        Duckles 67–844; Duckles 74–1280
About 1,200 items, in name order, mostly from the eighteenth and nineteenth centuries, with Italians predominating. Material listed includes photographs and portraits, letters, manuscript scores, and miscellaneous scraps (such as the few measures from *Tristan* that Wagner one day scribbled on some stationery). No actual illustrations.

0117   Beck, Sydney, and Elizabeth Roth. **Music in Prints**. New York: New York Public Library, 1965. unpaged. ML85 B34
Woodcuts, engravings, etchings, and lithographs showing musical activity, reproduced in black and white. Altogether, 52 scenes from the fifteenth century to 1959. Scholarly commentaries; index to instruments.

0118   Bernardi, Marziano, and Andrea Della Corte. **Gli Strumenti musicali nei dipinti della Galleria degli Uffizi**. Torino: Edizioni Radio Italiana, 1952. 177p. ML85 B4
        Duckles 67–897; Duckles 74–1240
Many major painters are found in this collection of 51 plates. The illustrations are annotated and keyed to a historical narrative. Index to instruments shown: there are 26 different ones.

0119   Besseler, Heinrich, and Max Schneider. **Musikgeschichte in Bildern**. Leipzig: VEB Deutscher Verlag für Music, 1961– (in progress). ML89 M9
        Duckles 67–295; Duckles 74–478-489
These volumes have appeared:

I/1. **Ozeanien**. Ed. Paul Collaer. 1965.

I/2. **Amerika: Eskimo und indianische Bevölkerung**. Ed. Paul Collaer *et al.* 1966.

II/1. **Ägypten**. Ed. Hans Hickmann. 1961.

II/4. **Griechenland**. Ed. Max Wegner. 1964.

II/5. **Etrurien und Rom**. Ed. Günter Fleischhauer. 1964.

II/7. **Alt-Amerika; Musik der Indianer in präkolumbischer Zeit**. Ed. Samuel Martí. 1970.

III/2. **Islam**. Ed. Henry George Farmer. 1966.

III/3. **Musikerziehung-Lehre und Theorie der Musik im Mittelalter**. Ed. Josef Smits van Waesberghe. 1969.

IV/1. **Oper-Szene und Darstellung von 1600 bis 1900**. Ed. H. C. Wolff. 1968.

IV/2. **Konzert; Öffentliche Musikdarbietung vom 17. bis 19. Jahrhundert**. Ed. Heinrich W. Schwab. n.d.

IV/3. **Haus- und Kammermusik** . . . Ed. Walter Salmen. 1969.

Each volume in this outstanding set contains from 150 to 200 black and white pictures, with historical background, commentaries, and citations to literature. Excellent chronologies are also found; e.g., the 60-page table in *Islam*, or the fine sequence of events in *Konzert*. Name indexes and bibliographies; maps and charts.

0120   Kinsky, Georg. **Geschichte der Musik in Bildern**. Leipzig: Breitkopf & Härtel, 1930. 364p. ML89 K55
         Duckles 67–330; Duckles 74–493
         Also published in English: *History of Music in Pictures* (London: Dent, 1930; reprint–New York: Dover, 1951), and in French: *Album musical* (Paris: Delagrave, 1930). All versions use the same plates, changing only text and indexes according to language. This pioneer work in iconography offered some 1,500 illustrations of persons, places, instruments, scores, and autographs. Kinsky let the pictures speak for themselves, without the elaborate analysis of socio-artistic implications that are now de rigueur in such compilations.

0121   Koch, Louis. **Katalog der Musikautographen Sammlung Louis Koch; Manuskripte, Briefe, Dokumente von Scarlatti bis Stravinsky**. Stuttgart: Hoffmannsche Buchdruckerei F. Krais, 1953. xxii, 361p. ML138 K63
         Duckles 67–1136
         Detailed description of 355 items from major composers (Handel, Bach, Haydn, Mozart, Beethoven, Schubert, etc., etc.), with references to literature, 21 facsimiles, and a name index.

0122   Komma, Karl. **Musikgeschichte in Bildern**. Stuttgart: Alfred Kröner, 1961. 332p. ML89 K72

Duckles 67–331; Duckles 74–494

Covers the entire span of music history with 743 excellent black and white pictures, source identifications, and careful commentaries. Index to personal names.

0123   Lang, Paul Henry, and Otto Bettmann. **A Pictorial History of Music.** New York: Norton, 1960. vii, 242p. ML89 L35
        Duckles 67–349; Duckles 74–495

An interesting group of pictures—most from the Bettmann Archive—rather ineffectively reproduced. They show people, scores, theatres, opera scenes, instruments. Commentary based on Lang's *Music in Western Civilization* (0100).

0124   Leppert, Richard David. **Musical Instruments and Performing Ensembles in Dutch Paintings of the 17th Century.** Unpublished Master's thesis, Indiana University, 1969. 214p.

Discusses 269 paintings by 58 artists: provenance, instruments depicted, ensemble questions. References to other catalogs.

0125   Lesure, François. **Iconographie musicale.** Genève: Éditions Minkoff, 1973– (in progress).
        Of ten projected volumes, these have appeared:

    I. Lesure, François. **L'Opéra classique française.** 1973. 120p. 100 illustrations; 34 in color. Extensive commentaries.
    II. Fromrich, Yane. **Musique et caricature in France au XIXe siècle.** 1973. 148p. 150 illustrations; 15 in color.

0126   Lesure, François. **Music in Art and Society.** University Park, Pa., London: Pennsylvania State University Press, 1968. ML85 L4813
        Duckles 74–496

Also available in the original German edition: *Musik und Gesellschaft im Bild* (Kassel: Bärenreiter, 1966). Pictures grouped in categories: the connoisseurs, the listeners, the music makers, the musicians of God. Elaborate commentaries bring out social contexts. English edition has 96 plates; German has 105. They illustrate paintings dating from the fourteenth century to 1807.

0127   Meyer, André. **Collection musicale André Meyer** . . . Abbeville: F. Paillart, 1961. 118, 295p. Supplement. Abbeville: F. Paillart, 1963. 16p. ML138 M5
        Duckles 67–1137; Duckles 74–1561

An illustrated (292 plates plus 10 in the Supplement) catalog of a major library of manuscripts, autographs, drawings, portraits, instruments. Arranged by composer or other person depicted. No index to artists.

0128   **Musikerhandschriften** . . . Hrsg. Walter Gerstenberg. Zürich: Atlantis Verlag, 1960-61. 2v. ML141 Z83 H44
        Duckles 67–783; Duckles 74–1090

English edition: *Composers' Autographs*, by Walter Gerstenberg and Martin Hürlimann (London: Cassel, 1968), 2v. Composers from Palestrina to Stravinsky are represented in 299 full-page facsimile plates of score pages in their handwriting. Discussion of sources, locations of the pages shown within the respective works, and bibliographic citations to other commentaries. More than a third of the composers are from the twentieth century.

0129   Naples. R. Conservatorio de Musica "S. Pietro a Majella." **Il Museo storico musicale di "S. Pietro a Majella."** Napoli: Giannini & Figli, 1930. vii, 153p. ML136 N15 C6
       Duckles 67–1022; Duckles 74–1399
    A listing of 734 items: portraits, instruments, busts, photos; and actual photographs of 155 of the items. Strongest in Italian musicians, many of whom are very little heard of today (Andreozzi, Anfossi, Broschi, etc.), but also much material on Bellini, and such odds and ends as a picture of Verdi's hand and Rossini's music stand.

0130   Parigi, Luigi. **La Musica nelle gallerie di Milano.** Milano: Perrella, 1935. 71p. (Studi Lombardi di Storia e d'Arte). ML85 P3 M8
       Duckles 67–1008; Duckles 74–1379
    Covers La Scala museum and five other galleries. Arrangement is by painter (mostly minor figures); very good descriptions and 21 illustrations. No index.

0131   Schaal, Richard. **Die Tonkünstler Porträts der Wiener Musiksammlung von Aloys Fuchs.** Wilhelmshaven: Heinrichshofen, 1970. 108p. (Quellenkataloge zur Musikgeschichte, 3). ML87 S3
    Reconstruction of a significant collection, now dispersed, of more than 2,000 portraits; 178 of them are reproduced. As many of the musicians included are now very obscure, this catalog is also useful as an identification tool: dates and musical metier are given for each person.

0132   Schünemann, Georg. **Musikerhandschriften von Bach bis Schumann.** Berlin, Zürich: Atlantis Verlag, 1936. 106p. ML96.4 S3 M8
    Duckles 67–799
    Drawn from the collection in the Berlin Staatsbibliothek; 96 facsimile plates with ample annotations.

0133   Vienna. Gesellschaft der Musikfreunde in Wien. **Geschichte der K. K. Gesellschaft der Musikfreunde in Wien** . . . Wien, A. Holzhausen, 1912. 2v. ML82 V4 G34
       Duckles 67–1105; Duckles 74–1512
    In the second volume there is an inventory of autographs and pictures. It is a large collection; e.g., for Haydn there are some 20 portraits listed and described. Also descriptions and some illustrations of 335 instruments in the museum.

0134   Vienna. Hoftheater. **Katalog der Portrait Sammlung** . . . Wien: Adolph W. Kunast, 1892-94. 3v.

Duckles 67—1106; Duckles 74—1515

Volume I contains a section on musicians: portraits of composers, singers, etc. The rest of the work is devoted to pictorial material on the theater.

0135   Winternitz, Emmanuel. **Musical Autographs from Monteverdi to Hindemith.** Princeton, N.J.: Princeton University Press, 1955. 2v. (Reprint, enlarged and corrected, with new preface—New York: Dover, 1965. 2v., pa.). ML96.4 W5
Duckles 67—807; Duckles 74—1112

Vol. I is an account of the history of musical writing, with an excellent bibliography. Vol. II consists of 196 plates, most of which had not already appeared in facsimile publication. Aims to demonstrate "some characteristic working and writing habits of particular Masters" in addition to providing a synopsis of notational style since 1600.

0136   Winternitz, Emmanuel. **Musical Instruments and Their Symbolism in Western Art.** New York: Norton; London: Faber & Faber, 1967. 240p. ML85 W58

Consists of 16 essays on iconology of instruments, considering their religious, erotic, and social meanings in diverse contexts. Illustrated by 225 halftones and 40 line drawings.

The search for a particular picture—of a certain person, or of a combination of elements in one scene—may often be resolved by consultation of works such as 0119, 0120, 0122, or 0125. But if these, or other books in this section, fail to bring results, the inquiry may well turn to materials noted earlier. MGG (0058) has more than 7,000 pictures; the Lavignac encyclopedia (0061) is a storehouse of unexpected drawings. The *Oxford Companion* (0064) is very well illustrated; Champlin's *Cyclopedia* (0066) features a large number of portraits, autographs, and facsimiles. The "Livre d'or" in 0072, the unusual photos of 0074, the drawings in 0076, the fine color plates in 0078 and 0081 and 0086, and, of course, *World Book* (0089): these are sources that place thousands of images before us. Then there are the illustrated histories, like Bernard (0094) and Bücken (0095). But if all else fails, there are still the unpublished resources—picture archives. The Bettmann Archive in New York is perhaps the best known collection of its kind; another large New York archive is that of the Freelance Photographers Guild ("world's largest agency for color photographs"). For a fee, one may request photos by topic, general or specific.

DIRECTORIES

The sources in this group have the character of "yellow pages" in a telephone book. Through one or another of these titles, we can locate a chime manufacturer, the name of a music school in Brussels, facts on the music collections in Irish libraries, the names of college flute teachers, the name of a concert series held in Akron, some agents who handle rock groups, disc jockeys in particular cities, etc., etc. Some directories are published annually, others less frequently or just one time; the annuals in this group differ from the ones found in the next section on the basis of content. An annual in the "Directories" section is an account of the musical *situation*, with respect to certain frame of inquiry; an annual in the "Annuals" section is a record of musical activity and research during a given year.

A number of old directories have been given space here—less for their current "yellow-page" value than for their historical perspective. A work such as 0139 preserves for us a slice of musical experience for its day, which breathes life into narrative history.

0137   Benton, Rita. **Directory of Music Research Libraries, including Contributors to the International Inventory of Musical Sources (RISM)**. Prelim. ed. Iowa City: University of Iowa, 1967-70. 2v. ML12 B45
Duckles 74—1139; Winchell 67—3BH19; ARBA 70—1222 (for Part 2)

One of the fine bibliographic projects of the International Association of Music Libraries, produced under Dr. Benton's direction in her role as President of the Commission of Research Libraries. Part 1 gives data on 333 libraries in Canada and the United States; Part 2 considers 784 libraries in 13 European countries: Austria, Belgium, Denmark, Finland, Germany (BRD and DDR), Great Britain, Ireland, Luxembourg, Netherlands, Norway, Sweden, and Switzerland. Further volumes are planned to cover other nations. Each library is described in terms of holdings, hours, rules for access, photoreproduction policy and equipment, literature about the library, and publications by the library. Names of librarians not given. No index in the North American volume; but the European part does have an index for each country through which one may locate special collections and find libraries under former names or names of parent institutions.

0138   **International Who Is Who in Music**. 5th (mid-century) ed. J. T. H. Mize, ed. Chicago: Who Is Who in Music, Inc., 1951. (1st ed. 1927). 576p. ML105 I5
Duckles 67—66; Duckles 74—86

Biographical guide to (primarily American) musicians of all sorts, with portraits. Many lists, for United States and Canada: music schools, periodicals, critics, orchestras, bands, opera companies, publishers, disc companies, instrument makers, and theme songs or signature melodies of 431 pop singers and bands. No longer published.

0139   **International Who's Who in Music and Musical Gazetteer**. . . . Ed. César Saerchinger. New York: Current Literature Publishing Co., 1918. 861p. ML105 S13
Duckles 67—67; Duckles 74—87

A biographical section is handy for tracing obscure musicians of the period; but the geographical arrangement of directory information is the essence of this volume. Under each country's name (and under major cities within a country) there are names of performers, conductors, teachers, critics, etc. There are lists of music schools, opera houses, orchestras (with conductors), and organizations. An excellent and fascinating cross-section of the music world after the Great War.

0140   **Jahrbuch der Musikwelt.** Bayreuth: J. Steeger, 1949. 696p. ML21
        J25
        Duckles 67—1309; Duckles 74—619
Despite the title, this was the only volume published. It is mainly focused on the period from 1945 to 1948, giving obituaries, European periodicals, German books, accounts of concerts and operas, etc., for those years. Directory data include an extensive census of music libraries by city (still useful as a supplement to 0137); also institutes and societies, music schools, orchestras, concert halls (with seating capacities, and six seating charts), publishers, music dealers, agents, performers, teachers. Since emphasis is European, it may be profitably used in partnership with 0138. No index.

0141   Lincoln, Harry B. **Directory of Music Faculties of American Colleges
        and Universities** ... 3rd ed. Binghamton, N.Y.: College Music
        Society, 1970. (1st ed. 1967). 695p. ML13 D57
        Duckles 74—177
An inventory of Canadian and U.S. music schools and departments, covering some 15,500 persons in 1,250 institutions. One section is made up of departmental descriptions (degrees offered, and faculty roster with teaching specialities and highest degrees held). A second section groups all faculty members by teaching areas; the final section is an alphabetical list of all the teachers.

0142   Macmillan, Keith. "Directory of National Music Centers." *Notes; the
        Quarterly Journal of the Music Library Association*, 27-4 (June
        1971), 680-93.
        Duckles 74—1819
Music Information Centers have been organized in many countries for the purposes of international cooperation, particularly with regard to exchange of material and provision of information on contemporary music. A group of these Centers form a Working Commission in the International Association of Music Libraries; these Centers are listed and described in the present directory. Addresses, history, objectives, organization, catalogs, publications, and services are outlined for Centers in Australia, Austria, Belgium, Canada, Czechoslovakia, Denmark, Finland, France, Germany (BRD), Iceland, Israel, Netherlands, Norway, Poland, Portugal, Sweden, Switzerland, United Kingdom, and the United States.

0143   **The Music Yearbook.** London: Macmillan; New York: St. Martin's,
        1972. 750p. ML21 M89483
        ARBA 73—1033
Essentially a British directory, with supplementary data for certain other countries. Organizations, performing groups of all kinds (arranged by city), festivals, periodicals, etc. May be used in conjunction with 0146, which is American in outlook.

0144   **Musical America: Directory Issue 1972.** Great Barrington, Mass.:
        Billboard Publications, 1972. 344p. ML12 M88
            Duckles 67–1310; Duckles 74–1826
        Began appearing under this title in 1968/69, superseding the annual
special directory issue of *High Fidelity/Musical America.* Coverage limited to
North America. Shows, by state: orchestras, series, chorales, theatre groups,
opera companies, festivals, music schools and departments, publishers,
managers, magazines, critics. An interesting capsule view of musical life in
various cities is also given. A good index to persons mentioned.

0145   **Musical Courier Annual Directory of the Concert World.** Evanston:
        Summy-Birchard, 1963– . ML13 M494
            Duckles 67–1312 (for 1963 ed.); Duckles 74–1825
        Earlier series, 1957-61. The 1963 volume carries a notice that it is
the "7th ed." Coverage of United States and Canada in the manner of 0144.

0146   **The Musician's Guide: The Directory of the World of Music, 1972.**
        New York: Music Information Service, Inc., 1972. (1st ed. 1954).
        1014p. ML13 M505
            Duckles 67–1311 (for 1957 ed.); Duckles 74–1827; ARBA 74–1092
        Primarily the United States and Canada, but world coverage in some
areas—e.g., festivals and competitions. Lists music schools, camps, 427
periodicals, 439 newspapers and magazines with music critics and record
reviewers, 218 music associations, 4,379 music publishers, foundations, 814
orchestras, 634 opera companies, etc. Also various prize winners (such as
Gold Recording, Country Music Hall of Fame), music teachers, managers,
instrument builders. Most comprehensive of the directories, but since it is not
published each year it must be used in conjunction with 0144 and/or
0145–and 0143 for the British data.

0147   **Official Talent and Booking Directory.** Los Angeles: Tolin Publish-
        ing Co., 1970– . ("published annually"). ML18 O3
        Issue examined was "California edition" of 1970. Groups, bands,
managers, agents, promoters, and other persons in the pop/rock music
business. Interesting inventory of radio stations and their "formats," TV
shows that feature certain "talent," music dealers, recording studios. Most
thorough treatment of these aspects.

0148   **Purchaser's Guide to the Music Industries.** New York: The Music
        Trades, 1897– . (annual). ML18 P9
            Duckles 67–1315; Duckles 74–1831
        Title varies, but publication has persisted; latest seen was 1971,
"75th annual issue." Lists of piano, organ, chime, and other instrument
manufacturers; tuners and technicians; music merchandise manufacturers and
wholesalers. Valuable descriptive list of publishers. Trade marks of the music
industry. Does not list performers.

0149   **Who's Who in Music: And Musicians' International Directory**. 6th
        ed. New York: Hafner, 1972. (1st ed. 1935). 498p. ML106 G7 W44
        Duckles 67—91 (for 4th ed.); Duckles 74—135; ARBA 73—1044

Another national directory in international clothing: this is 90
percent British. Good descriptions of about 50 music schools and performing
organizations; plus sections on agents, impresarios, festivals, opera companies,
old music dealers, music journals—nearly all U.K. except for some 20 pages of
overseas entries. (The foreign information cannot be trusted; at any rate the
survey of orchestras in Ohio omits the Cleveland Orchestra.) There is a very
long train of British biographical sketches, around 5,000 in all. Some
foreigners are included, but they are treated cursorily.

ANNUALS

0150   **Americana Annual**. New York: Americana Corp., 1923— . (annual).
        AE5 E364
        Winchell 67—AD8

0151   **Britannica Book of the Year**. Chicago: Encyclopaedia Britannica,
        1938— . (annual). AE5 E364
        Winchell 67—AD9

0150 and 0151 are similar enough to be discussed together. Each is
intended both to supplement its respective encyclopedia and to form a record
of events for the past year. (Note that the events presented are of the year
prior to the year of the title.) The "Music" article in each book presents a
synthesis of important activity in the realms of serious and popular music, on
a world-wide base, but strongest for the United States. Taken as a historical
series, either set offers a remarkable panorama of changing musical life. As
the record of a single year, either annual gives names of winners in
competitions, important debuts and premieres, best-selling recordings,
changes in significant positions (e.g., orchestra directorships), and much news
of the pop world. Both volumes are carefully indexed, and one may locate
facts on musical matters in various articles.

0152   **Jahrbuch der Musikbibliothek Peters**. Leipzig: C. F. Peters,
        1894-1940. (annual). (Reprint—New York: Kraus, 1965). ML5 J15
        Duckles 67—453; Duckles 74—585
        Continued by:
        Deutsches Jahrbuch der Musikwissenschaft. Leipzig: Edition Peters,
        1956— . (annual).

While the principal content of these yearbooks is scholarly essays,
issues do carry a useful "Rückblick" of the previous year—referring to
birthdays of musicians and giving obituaries. Dissertations and other
university papers are also listed. An index to books on music from various
countries, carried in the original *Jahrbuch*, was continued as the *Bibliographie
der Musikschriftums* (0259).

0153   **Pierre Key's Music Year Book** . . . **1924-38.** New York: Pierre Key,
Inc., 1925-38. 6v. ML13 P52
    Duckles 67—1314; Duckles 74—1830
.Vol. 1, 1925/26: some general surveys—e.g., "Music in Spain"; list of
music societies; musical activity in 11 U.S. cities; lists of U.S. and foreign
orchestras and opera companies (with conductors and singers identified); U.S.
music schools with their faculties named; lists of performers of all sorts with
addresses and biographies of some of them. Vol. 2, 1926/27: same kind of
facts as Vol. 1, plus lists of premieres, concert halls, critics, journals, and
publishers (all international). Vol. 3, 1928, and Vol. 4, 1929/30: same
format. Vol. 5, 1935: all-U.S.A. issue, covering the same categories as earlier
volumes but adding dancers, bands, collections of musical instruments,
lecturers, and personnel lists of major orchestras. Vol. 6, 1938: also covers
U.S.A., similar to Vol. 5; includes a special article on music planned for the
New York World's Fair of 1939.

0154   Whitaker, Joseph. **Almanack; 1869—** . London: Whitaker, 1869—.
(annual). 1973 ed.: xx, 1220p. AY754 W5
    Winchell 67—CG109
Information on musical organizations and activities included, with
emphasis on British Commonwealth nations.

0155   **World Almanac and Book of Facts, 1868—** . New York: Newspaper
Enterprise Association, 1868— . (annual). AY67 N5 W7
    Winchell 67—CG55
Publisher varies. Most useful of the general almanacs; American
emphasis. Considerable information on music—e.g., 1973 edition gives current
Broadway and London plays (including musicals) with number of performances; names, addresses, and conductors of Canadian and U.S. orchestras; Canadian and U.S. opera companies; data on most popular recordings.
Earlier editions have given names of operas performed by the various
companies. Dates and brief identifications for composers and performers.

Almanacs are numerous. Another good American model is the
Information Please Almanac (1947—), with many facts on the order of 0155.
Many other countries have such annual compendia, concentrating on national
data: e.g., the French *Almanach Hachette* (1894—). Editors of these works
are quite self-conscious about keeping up to date, so their products are
generally dependable aids in mundane inquiries like names of contest winners
or whether a certain musician has passed on to the heavenly chorale. Winchell
is a good starting point for finding them.

MISCELLANEOUS

0156   Alexander, Franz. **Zitatenschatz der Musik; 1000 Aphorismen,
Sprüche, Sprichwörter** . . . Leipzig: F. Ahrens Nachf. C. Z. Zierow,
1936. 151p. ML66 A37 Z5

Aphorisms, proverbs, quotations on music and musicians (18 quotes about J. S. Bach, for instance—by Goethe, Beethoven, Wagner, Bülow, etc.); 1,023 items in all. Quotes are translated into German, and organized by key word; hence, a bit awkward to locate specific statements from other languages. Name index and subject index will help in the effort.

While 0156 and 0161 concentrate on musical quotations, it should be remembered that there are also some very large general quotation dictionaries—in which quotes about musical subjects appear in profusion. Principal among them are Bartlett and Stevenson:

0157   Bartlett, John. **Familiar Quotations**. 14th ed., rev. and enl. by Emily M. Beck. Boston: Little, 1968. (1st ed. 1855). 1750p. PN6081 B27
        Winchell 67—BD75
Arranged by author of the quotation. Outstanding index of more than 117,000 entries permits facile access. Beyond "music" itself, there are quotations about singing, various instruments and other aspects of the art. At least one poet even mentioned the Dorian mode: "Anon they move/ In perfect phalanx, to the Dorian mood/ Of flutes and soft recorders" (Paradise Lost I-549).

0158   Stevenson, Burton Egbert. **Home Book of Quotations, Classical and Modern**. 10th ed. New York: Dodd, 1967. (1st ed. 1934). 2816p. PN6081 S73
        Winchell 67—BD83
Arranged by topic, with author index, which makes it somewhat quicker to find remarks pertaining to music. More than 50,000 quotations included. About 150 are found under "Music," with many more under various related headings.

0159   Berkowitz, Freda Pastor. **Popular Titles and Subtitles of Musical Compositions**. New York: Scarecrow Press, 1962. 182p. ML113 B39
        Duckles 67—607; Duckles 74—799
List of 502 titles associated with serious compositions, from the seventeenth to the twentieth centuries, with explanations. Some of these are readily found in various music dictionaries (like "Moonlight"), but others would cause some trouble (like "Bucolic Sonata"). Composer index.

0160   Collaer, Paul, and Albert Van der Linden. **Historical Atlas of Music**: **A Comprehensive Study of the World's Music, Past and Present**. Trans. Allan Miller. Cleveland: World, 1968. 175p. ML160 C68
        Duckles 67—313; Duckles 74—490
Same maps and plates as in the original edition, *Atlas historique de la musique* (Paris: Elsevier, 1960). Attractive and scholarly geographic perspective on musical development.

0161   Cullen, Marion Elizabeth. **Memorable Days in Music**. Metuchen, N.J.: Scarecrow Press, 1970. v, 233p. ML13 C84

A compilation of musical quotations and a synopsis of events in music history arranged in calendar sequence. (On January 2, Tito Schipa was born—in 1889—and Glenn Gould made his American debut—in 1955.)

0162 **Facts on File: A Weekly World News Digest with Cumulative Index.** New York: Facts on File, 1940— . (weekly; annual bound volumes). D10 F3
Winchell 67—DA51
A classified summary of events in the world, emphasizing the United States. Cumulative indexes, culminating in five-year indexes, make it easy to locate specific items. This seems to be the only reference weekly that gives systematic attention to musical events. Notice is taken of premieres, awards, obituaries, opera and musical theatre performances, and new publications of major composers.

0163 Fuld, James J. **The Book of World-Famous Music, Classical, Popular and Folk.** 2d ed. New York: Crown Publishers, 1971. xiii, 688p. ML113 F8
Duckles 67—718 (for 1966 ed.); Duckles 74—960; ARBA 72—1081
Analyzes the publishing past of 704 familiar melodies, with allusions to early performances and recordings as well as biographical accounts of composers, authors, and performers. Melodies are given, in original key, with text incipits. Extensive supplementary material about music publishing, with plate number lists for Jurgen and Ricordi. A scholarly and intriguing work.

0164 **Guinness Book of World Records.** Ed. by Norris McWhirter and Ross McWhirter. 11th ed. New York: Sterling, 1972. (1st ed. 1955). 640p. AG243 G87
ARBA 71—180 (for 1970 ed.)
Musical facts under various headings throughout: world's smallest violin, tallest opera house, longest operatic cadenza, most monotonous song, and highest pitch (60 billion vibrations per second!). No documentation for these records, however; one must do some searching to locate verifications. The index is poor.

0165 **Hinrichsen's Musical Year Book, 1944—** .London: Hinrichsen, 1944— . (irregular). ML21 H65
Duckles 67—1308; Duckles 74—1821
Began life as an annual, with attention to events of the preceding year (e.g., accounts of London concerts 1943-44, 1944-45 appear in the issue for 1945/46; obituaries listed, etc.), but transformed into collection of essays—some quite valuable—by musicologists. Seems to have suspended publication with *Hinrichsen's Eleventh Music Book: Music Libraries and Instruments; Papers Read at the Joint Congress, Cambridge 1959, of the International Association of Music Libraries and the Galpin Society* (1961). That volume contains a cumulative index to the whole set.

0166   Leipoldt, Friedrich. **Von wem und was ist das?**... Hildesheim:
        F. M. Hörhold, 1953, 372p. ML102 L4
        Some 3,500 titles of compositions are the principal value of this
volume. Identification of many obscure works, including operas, operettas,
instrumental pieces and ballets, is made possible. This and the following item
are excellent starting points for who-wrote-this? searches.

0167   Quarry, W. Edmund. **Dictionary of Musical Compositions and
        Composers**. London: Routledge, 1920? viii, 192p. ML105 Q8
        Useful for title entries, which encompass instrumental works,
choruses, songs, and operas—with listings of individual arias. No operettas.
Titles given in language considered most suitable for British readers, but
sometimes in several languages; arias in original language.

CHAPTER 3

UNIVERSAL BIOGRAPHICAL SOURCES

Facts about famous musicians are easy to find; many of the encyclopedic works already cited (0058-0090) present a plentiful harvest of such data. Indeed, persons who are not so well known can often be studied via MGG and other encyclopedias. The need for more sources becomes evident when we encounter names that are really obscure—perhaps entirely unknown—outside of certain narrow contexts. In the present work, appropriate sources of biographical data (on minor figures as well as the great masters) are set forth in categories: universal, national, and topical. Universal sources deal with musicians of all sorts and nationalities: these are listed in this volume. National sources are limited to persons from given countries: these appear in the second volume. Finally, there are topical sources— musicians grouped by their instrument (e.g., pianists) or other common characteristic (e.g., jazz players): these are discussed in the third volume.

INDEXES AND GUIDES

The immensity of biographical literature calls for an index apparatus. Among the numerous efforts to simplify access to biographies, the items that follow appear to be most widely useful.

0168   Arnim, Max. **Internationale Personalbibliographie** . . . 2. verb. und stark verm. Aufl. Leipzig: Hiersemann, 1944-63. (1st ed. 1936). 3v. Z8001 A1 A7
       Winchell 67—AA11
     A list of bibliographies about people, gathered from books, journals, Festschriften and miscellaneous publications. Since bibliographies are often published with biographical material, Arnim can also be used to locate such sketches. Some 90,000 names are treated.

0169   **Biography Index: A Cumulative Index to Biographical Material in Books and Magazines.** New York: H. W. Wilson, 1946— . (quarterly; annual and triennial cumulations). Z5301 B5
       Winchell 67—AJ2
     Each issue covers biographical writing in some 1,700 periodicals, current numbers; and also in recent books in English; plus *New York Times* obituaries. Persons from all times and countries will be found listed, as long as they are subjects of current articles or books. Alphabetical main section, with a handy index to professions or occupations that includes various musical designations.

0170   Bull, Storm. **Index to Biographies of Contemporary Composers**. New York: Scarecrow Press, 1964. 405p. ML105 B9
      Duckles 67—405; Duckles 74—646
Locates biographical information in 69 different sources, and arranges the entries by composer. Limited to twentieth century musicians.

0171   Hyamson, Albert. **A Dictionary of Universal Biography of All Ages and of All Peoples**. 2d ed. New York: Dutton, 1951. (1st ed. 1916). 679p. CT103 H9
      Winchell 67—AJ5
Indexes 24 large biographical compilations.

0172   Phillips, Lawrence Barnett. **Dictionary of Biographical Reference; Containing over 100,000 Names** . . . 3rd ed. London: Low; Philadelphia: Gebbie, 1889. (1st ed. 1871). 1038p. CT103 P5
      Winchell 67—AJ9
Covers some 40 biographical collections.

0173   Riches, Phyllis M. **Analytical Bibliography of Universal Collected Biography, Comprising Books Published in the English Tongue** . . . London: The Library Association, 1934. 709p. Z5301 R53
      Winchell 67—AJ10
Similar to 0171 and 0172, but including two fresh approaches: a chronological list of the biographees and also a grouping of them by profession.

        Other indexes of this type are cited in Winchell. In addition, there are various works of wider scope that are useful for locating biographies: almost all the periodical indexes, for example; plus a few less obvious titles like *Essay and General Literature Index* (0360) and the British Museum *General Catalogue of Printed Books* (0241).
        These items are indirect sources that serve to lead one to a place where actual biographical facts appear. But it should be mentioned that many of the direct sources serve also as indirect guides to other biographical writing; e.g., a biography in MGG, or in Baker's *Biographical Dictionary* (0175) will carry references to longer or more specialized studies of the person discussed. Library catalogs and various types of bibliographies—treated in Chapter 4—may also function in this manner.
        Volumes IV and V of the present work will recognize the principal individual biographies on prominent musicians.
        Now we shall examine the most useful collections of biographical studies having international coverage: some exclusively musical, others more general, but with significant musical inclusions.

COLLECTED BIOGRAPHIES OF INTERNATIONAL SCOPE

0174   Abert, Hermann J. **Illustriertes Musik-Lexikon**. Stuttgart: J. Engel-
horns Nachf., 1927. 542p. ML100 A2
     Duckles 67–1; Duckles 74–1
While there are terminological entries in this dictionary, it is of use
today for its biographical articles. Range of inclusion is wide, writing is
intelligent (by several prominent musicologists in addition to Abert) though
not ponderous. Some bibliographic citations; 503 pictures.

0175   Baker, Theodore. **Biographical Dictionary of Musicians**. 5th ed.,
completely rev. by Nicolas Slonimsky. New York: G. Schirmer,
1958. (1st ed. 1900). xv, 1855p. Supplement, by Nicolas Slonimsky.
New York: G. Schirmer, 1971. 262p. ML105 B16
     Duckles 67–51; Duckles 74–65
The most useful and reliable work of its kind. Concise, scholarly
entries with bibliographies of writings by and about the persons included
along with lists of compositions. No pictures. The 1971 Supplement, which
supersedes the 1965 Supplement, gives added emphasis to avant-garde
composers as well as popular and folk artists. Although not free from error
(cf. review in *Notes*, 29/2, Dec. 1972, 253-54) accuracy of dates and other
information is at a very high level.

0176   Bingley, William. **Musical Biography; Memoirs of the Lives and
Writings of the Most Eminent Musical Composers and Writers Who
Have Flourished in the Different Countries of Europe during the
Last Three Centuries**. 2d ed. London: R. Bentley, 1834. (1st ed.
1822). 2v. (Reprint–New York: Da Capo Press, 1971). (Da Capo
Press Music Reprint Series). ML385 B61
     ARBA 72–1136
A semi-popular compilation of marginal value today, but valuable
for facts on luminaries of a century and a half past. Emphasis on Englishmen.
Some detailed lists of works.

0177   Bonaccorsi, Alfredo. **Nuovo dizionario musicale Curci**. Milano:
Curci, 1954. 557p. ML100 B835
     Duckles 67–7; Duckles 74–6
A good cross-section of musical personalities at mid-century. Strong
in coverage of musicologists. Bibliographies, lists of works, and modern
editions.

0178   Brown, James Duff. **Biographical Dictionary of Musicians**. Paisley,
London: A. Gardner, 1886. (Reprint–Hildesheim: Georg Olms,
1970). ML105 B87
     Duckles 74–68
More than 4,000 brief but informative articles, on persons from all
times and places. Partial lists of works. No pictures. Good starting point for
basic searches on lesser figures of the nineteenth century.

0179   Brown, James Duff, and Stephen S. Stratton. **British Musical Biography: A Dictionary of Musical Artists, Authors and Composers, Born in Britain and in Its Colonies.** London: Reeves, 1897. ii, 471p. (Reprint—New York: Da Capo Press, 1971). (Da Capo Press Music Reprint Series). ML106 G7 B8
        Duckles 67–88; Duckles 74–129; ARBA 72–1137
    Excellent source of facts on obscure musicians, who are deliberately given space in preference to the nobles of the standard repertoire. Lists of works, notice of first performances and debuts. About 5,000 entries.

0180   Carlson, Effie B. **A Bio-Bibliographical Dictionary of Twelve-Tone and Serial Composers.** Metuchen, N.J.: Scarecrow Press, 1970. 233p. ML105 C39
        Duckles 74–69; Winchell 67–3BH10; ARBA 71–1230
    For each of 80 composers we have biographical information and lists of works; latter are limited to piano compositions only. Bibliographies by composer and also of writings about serial music.

0181   Choron, Alexandre, et F. J. M. Fayolle. **Dictionnaire historique des musiciens, artistes et amateurs, morts ou vivans** . . . Paris: Valade, 1810-11. 2v. (Reprint—Hildesheim: Georg Olms, 1971). ML105 C55
        Duckles 67–52; Duckles 74–70
    A pioneer French compilation which gives a sweeping perspective over the international scene of its time. Concise entries, with some lists of works; no documentation. Formed the basis for 0202.

0182   **Compositores de América; Datos biográficas y catálogos de sus obras.** Washington: Organización de los Estados Americanos, 1955– .
        Duckles 67–117; Duckles 74–156
    Sixteen volumes issued through 1970. Most volumes treat a dozen or so composers from diverse nations of North and South America. Biographical sketches, portraits; classified lists of works with timing and instrumentation; pages from scores; reference to recordings. No general index, but each volume gives contents of all earlier volumes.

0183   Cummings, William H. **Biographical Dictionary of Musicians.** London: Novello, n.d.; preface dated 1892. 84p. ML105 C97
    Very brief identifications, useful for minor names. Also some interesting findings in a list of "ages of eminent deceased musicians," which arranges those persons from youngest to oldest (age at death). Pergolesi emerges as the significant composer with the shortest life—26 years—while Auber lived longest (89 years).

0184   **Current Biography.** New York: H. W. Wilson Co., 1940– . (quarterly). (monthly; annual cumulations). CT100 C8
        Winchell 67–AJ28
    Selects some 300 to 400 persons annually—people in the news—for detailed coverage. The articles present a personal kind of information not

ordinarily available: color of eyes, height, favorite books, etc., etc.; and often quotations from the biographee. Portraits, bibliographies. Excellent retrospective indexing scheme; updated material (e.g., obituaries) appears in later issues after an article is published. Occupation index will locate musicians, who are quite well represented.

0185   **Dictionary of International Biography.** Cambridge, London, and Dartmouth: Melrose Press, Limited, 1963– . (annual). CT101 D5
Useful for attention to persons of second-line importance as well as leading names. Universal coverage. The tenth edition (1973) includes 20,000 sketches in its four volumes. Over ten years, some 100,000 people have been in at least one of the editions; they are all listed in a master-index that is part of the tenth edition. Musicians are well represented.

0186   **Dizionario Ricordi della musica e dei musicisti.** Direttore: Claudio Sartori; redattori: Fausto Broussard, *et al.* Milano: Ricordi, 1959. xii, 1155p. ML100 D65
        Duckles 67–14; Duckles 74–13
A very good general cumulation of sketches, including popular composers and writers on music. Lists of works; bibliographies.

0187   Eitner, Robert. **Biographisch-bibliographisches Quellen-Lexikon der Musiker und Musikgelehrten der christlichen Zeitrechnung bis zur Mitte des neunzehnten Jahrhunderts.** Leipzig: Breitkopf & Härtel, 1900-1904. 10v. (Reprint–New York: Musurgia, 1947). ML105 E37
        Duckles 67–55, 760, 782, 786; Duckles 74–74
One of the great efforts in music bibliography, intended as a locator of primary sources on pre-1800 music. Data on lives of composers is given with lists of works—published and not—with European library locations. Supplements and corrections included in the reprint edition. Being superseded by 0419.

0188   Etude Music Magazine. **Portraits . . . of the World's Best-Known Musicians . . .** Compiled and edited by Guy McCoy. Philadelphia: Theodore Presser, 1946. 251p. ML87 E78
        Duckles 67–56; Duckles 74–75
Small pictures of 4,748 persons, from past and more recent times, with brief identifications. Geographical index, by state, for Americans. Good source for finding out what someone rather obscure looked like.

0189   Ewen, David. **Composers since 1900: A Biographical and Critical Guide.** New York: H. W. Wilson Co., 1969. 639p. ML390 E883
        Duckles 74–79; Winchell 67–3BH12
Supersedes three earlier compilations by Ewen: *Composers of Today*; *American Composers Today*; and *European Composers Today*. Popular-style biographies with lists of works and discussions of them. Considerable detail which, for lesser figures, is difficult to locate elsewhere.

0190   Ewen, David. **Great Composers, 1300-1900: A Biographical and Critical Guide**. New York: H. W. Wilson Co., 1966. 429p. ML105 E944

Winchell 67–1BH12

Supersedes the author's *Composers of Yesterday*. Format similar to that of 0189; covers some 200 persons.

0191   Fétis, François Joseph. **Biographie universelle des musiciens et bibliographie générale de la musique**. 2me. éd. Paris: Firmin Didot Frères, Fils et Cie, 1860-66. (1st ed. 1835-44). 8v. Supplément: éd. Arthur Pougin. Paris: Didot, 1878-80. 2v. ML105 F42

Duckles 67–61; Duckles 74–81

Bio-bibliographical essays of detailed and critical nature; lists of works. A great pioneering effort by one of the earliest scholarly biographers in music. Fétis did not aim at critical objectivity, however; nor was he meticulous in checking facts. Sources for corrections and additions are cited in Coover (0048).

0192   Fisher, Renee B. **Musical Prodigies**. New York: Association Press, 1973. 240p. ML81 F58

ARBA 74–1083

Around 440 persons have been selected for their precocity, and some account is given of their early musical experiences. An uneven, popular style pervades these brief notices, but some interesting anecdotes emerge (such as that of the six-year-old Albeniz auditioning for admission to the Paris Conservatory: he threw away his chances, literally, by tossing a ball into a mirror). Jazz, pop, and classical artists are included.

0193   Gerber, Ernst Ludwig. **Neues historisch-biographisches Lexikon der Tonkünstler**... Leipzig: A. Kühnel, 1812-14. 4v. (Reprint, hrsg. von Othmar Wessely–Graz: Akademische Druck- u. Verlagsanstalt, 1966). ML105 G38

Duckles 67–63; Duckles 74–82

The first edition, *Historisch-biographisches Lexikon der Tonkünstler*..., was published in two volumes (Leipzig: J. G. I. Breitkopf, 1790-92). Earliest large-scale biographical compilation, based on Walther (0055). Brief identifications to full-column treatments of European musicians, instrument makers, publishers, and writers. Some lists of works. Second edition omits some names from the first; both should be consulted for full coverage, and fortunately the reprint version has both (with some later corrections. Further addenda, by J. F. Reichardt and by F. S. Kandler, are cited by Coover in 0048). *Anhang* cites drawings, engravings, carvings, busts, and statues of musicians, with locations; also engravings of famous organs.

0194   Goodman, Alfred A. **Musik von A-Z**. München: Südwest Verlag, 1971. vi, 648p. ML100 G67

Universal, up-to-date biographical sketches with portraits for serious and pop/rock/jazz musicians. Thorough coverage.

0195   Häusler, Josef. **Musik im 20. Jahrhundert; von Schönberg zu Penderecki.** Bremen: Schünemann, 1969. 441p. ML197 H17 M9
Discussions of 56 composers, centering on style of their works and on their aesthetic ideas. Introductory essay on modern trends.

0196   Honegger, Marc. **Dictionnaire de la musique.** Paris: Bordas, 1970— . (in progress). ML100 D65
    Duckles 74—25
Two of three planned volumes have appeared, under the title "Les hommes et leurs oeuvres." Following these biographical compilations will be a volume on "Science de la musique." M. Honegger, assisted by at least 180 collaborators, has provided a competent universal set of facts which include lists of works and some bibliographical references.

0197   "Index to Musical Necrology," in *Notes; the Quarterly Journal of the Music Library Association*, 1966— . ML27 U5 M695
This list of persons who died in the previous year has been a regular feature in June issues since 1966. References to published obituaries and further biographical information are given.

0198   **Malá encyklopédia hudby.** Sprac.: Kol. autorov pod ved. Mariána Juříka. Predslov: Ladislav Mokrý. 1. vyd. Bratislava: Obzor, t. Pravda, 1969. 642p. ML100 M17
    Duckles 74--31
International biographical entries with numerous little photos. Popular and classical artists. Particularly useful for Eastern European musicians included. (Musical terms are also found, but this aspect of the book is not of much value.)

0199   Mattheson, Johann. **Grundlage einer Ehren-Pforte, woran der tüchtigsten Capellmeister, Componisten, Musikgelehrten, Tonkünstler, etc. Leben, Wercke, Verdienste, etc., erscheinen sollen . . .** Vollst. originalgetreuer Neudruck mit gelegentlichen bibliographischen Hinweisen und Matthesons Nachträgen, hrsg. Max Schneider. Berlin: Leo Liepmannssohn, 1910. (1st ed. 1740). xliv, 428p. (Reprint— Kassel: Bärenreiter, 1969; Graz: Akademische Druck- u. Verlagsanstalt, 1969). ML105 M42
    Duckles 67—69; Duckles 74—90
These 137 biographical articles comprised the first self-contained work of musical biography. Sketches vary from a paragraph to several pages in length, giving many insights into the musical world at the peak of the baroque. Handel, Froberger, and Telemann were there, with such lesser colleagues as Almende, Argyropylus, and Avenorius—but J. S. Bach was among the missing. Schneider's edition (of the original 1740 printing) has marginal glosses throughout. A rare feature in early biographies: most of the pieces were written by the subjects themselves. Possibly JSB was left out because he did not bother to return his questionnaire.

0200   Merseburger, Carl. **Kurzgefasstes Tonkünstlerlexikon für Musiker und Freunde der Musik** . . . Neu bearbeitet und ergänzt von Wilhelm Altmann. 14. stark erweiterte Aufl. Regensburg: G. Bosse, 1936. (1st ed. 1860, as P. Frank, *Kleines Tonkünstlerlexikon*). 730p. (Reprint, as "15. Auflage"–Wilhelmshaven: Heinrichshofens Verlag, 1971–). ML105 M47

        Duckles 67–70 (for 1936 ed.); Duckles 74–91

More than 21,000 persons in all areas of music are given brief identifications (Beethoven a paragraph; others mostly one or two lines). A useful feature is listing of pen names, under the pseudonym itself; e.g., Frank, Paul = Merseburger, Carl. The 1971 reprint makes no alteration in the 1936 edition, but is offered as the first of a two-volume set, with the second volume providing international update.

0201   Prieberg, Fred K. **Lexikon der neuen Musik.** München: K. Alber, 1958. x, 494p. ML105 P74

        Duckles 67–74; Duckles 74–96

Half- to full-page accounts of more than 700 twentieth-century composers. Many works are cited, but not in systematic lists. Numerous autograph signatures reproduced; also facsimiles of scores. No portraits. A topic/title index makes it possible to see who wrote hundreds of obscure works; however, not every title from the text appears in the index, and one should note that most titles must be located in their German translations.

0202   Sainsbury, John S. **A Dictionary of Musicians from the Earliest Ages to the Present Time, Comprising the Most Important Biographical Contents of the Works of Gerber, Choron and Fayolle, Count Orloff, Dr. Burney, Sir John Hawkins, etc.** . . . London: Sainsbury, 1824. 2v. (Reprint, with introduction by Henry George Farmer–New York: Da Capo Press, 1966. 2v.). (Da Capo Press Music Reprint Series). ML105 S2

        Duckles 67–54; Duckles 74–73

Based on 0181, with other material from 0096, 0098, 0193. However, Sainsbury gave an English emphasis to his gathering by condensing continental biographies and adding a hundred new self-authored sketches by Englishmen. Anecdotal style.

0203   **Sohlmans Musiklexikon: nordiskt och allmänt uppslagsverk för tonkonst, musikliv och dans.** Stockholm: Sohlman, 1948-52. 4v. ML100 S66

        Duckles 67–43; Duckles 74–56

There are terms and subject articles in this encyclopedia, but the principal worth of it is biographical. Good coverage of contemporaries, strongest for Scandinavians but useful for lesser figures elsewhere. Lists of works; writings about the composers. Article authors identified. Portraits.

0204   Spemanns, Wilhelm. **Spemanns goldenes Buch der Musik** . . . Neue Aufl. Stuttgart: W. Spemann, 1912. (1st ed. 1900). 973p. ML100 S74

Most useful for the section on contemporary composers, which presents portraits and short biographies of more than 600 persons. Also a valuable quick-identification section on earlier musicians, replete with nineteenth century obscurities.

0205 Thompson, Kenneth. **St. Martin's Dictionary of Twentieth-Century Composers (1911-1971).** New York: St. Martin's Press, 1973. 666p. ML118 T5
    ARBA 74—1107

Actually considers only 32 persons, who met criteria of being extremely influential and also deceased. Brief biographies; very detailed chronological lists of works (with timing, instrumentation, first performance and publication facts, bibliographic citations) and selective—quite uneven— bibliographies on each composer. Those included are Bartók, Berg, Bloch, Busoni, Debussy, Delius, Elgar, deFalla, Fauré, Hindemith, Holst, Honegger, Ives, Janáček, Kodály, Mahler, Martinů, Nielsen, Poulenc, Prokofiev, Puccini, Rachmaninov, Ravel, Roussel, Satie, Schönberg, Sibelius, Strauss, Stravinsky, Varèse, Vaughan Williams, and Webern. Numerous errors and omissions mar the usefulness of this handy cumulation.

A few other works may be mentioned for their occasional utility in musical biography, although virtually all their contents are covered by sources cited above. One is the great *Biographie universelle*, usually identified as "Michaud," issued in 45 volumes from 1843 to 1865 (Winchell 67—AJ13). Other works of impressive scope are the *Nouvelle biographie générale . . . ,* usually cited as "Hoefer," comprising 46 volumes published from 1853 to 1866 (Winchell 67—AJ20) and Oettinger's *Moniteur des dates,* a nine-volume collection of some 100,000 identifications (Winchell 67—AJ21). There are a number of "who's who" publications that cross national boundaries—none as good for musicians as 0185, but sometimes rewarding—such as *International Who's Who* (Winchell 67—AJ29), *Who's Who* (covering British Commonwealth; Winchell 67—AJ155), or *Middle East and North Africa* (Winchell 67—CI41).

CHAPTER 4

GUIDES TO OTHER SOURCES OF INFORMATION
IN GENERAL CATEGORIES

The long title of this section might be expressed concisely as "bibliography," but only at the cost of some clarity. In music, a bibliography may be a list of compositions, a list of treatises on music, a list of writings about certain composers or their compositions, a list of recordings; indeed, the term bibliography is properly applied also to studies of music printing and related topics; and to the art of careful description of scores, manuscripts, and unusual materials. In still another sense, music bibliography is taken to mean the study of information sources of all types—exactly the scope of the present book.

Hopefully, the title selected is unequivocal. In this section we examine pathfinders, signposts, and beacons that lead to desired information. To say that they point to "general categories" means only that they are concerned with wide areas of musical information rather than single topics only. A fair analogy may be drawn with the previous chapter on collected biographies; the items in that chapter took in sizeable groups of musicians, rather than individuals apart. In fact, the "direct information sources" of Chapter 2 are also general in focus. In all of these generalized chapters, information is available on very narrow, specific topics—but it tends to be extremely limited information. Where more information on such a topic is needed, the specialized chapters of subsequent volumes should be engaged as appropriate pathfinders.

BIBLIOGRAPHIES OF BIBLIOGRAPHIES

If one bibliography is a guide to certain sources of information, another may well be a guide to other guides . . . a bibliography of guides, a bibliography of bibliographies. Just as a type of bibliography exists that lists other bibliographies, there also exist a few works at the next higher power: those that list bibliographies of bibliographies. That is the function of the present chapter.

We begin suitably with the greatest compilation of bibliographic lists.

0206   Besterman, Theodore. **A World Bibliography of Bibliographies and of Bibliographical Catalogues, Calendars, Abstracts, Digests, Indexes, and the Like.** 4th ed., rev. and greatly enlarged. Lausanne: Societas Bibliographica, 1965-66. (1st ed. 1939-40). 5v. Z1002 B5685
Winchell 67–1AA3

The author defines a bibliography as a "list of books arranged according to some permanent principle"; thus excluding library and bookseller catalogues (for lack of permanent principle), and lists of artworks, music scores, or whatever is not a book. He also omits bibliographies that are found in journals or as parts of larger works–that is, he restricts himself to lists that were separately published. Despite these limitations, some 117,000 titles have been discovered to fit the criteria. These are grouped under some 16,000 headings and subheadings–including "music" (about 700 items) and various related topics (opera, chamber music, etc.). Scope is international, though coverage is better in the more familiar European languages (Besterman confesses to some uneasiness with the "finno-ugric" family). An estimate of the number of entries in each work cited has been provided. There is an author-title index.

0207 **Bibliographic Index: A Cumulative Bibliography of Bibliographies**. New York: H. W. Wilson Co., 1938– . (semiannual; annual cumulation). Z1002 B594
       Winchell 67–AA14
       A most valuable complement to Besterman, this index covers current publication of bibliographies whether separately published or found in periodicals or as parts of larger works. Universal coverage, but strongest in English language material. As many as 1,500 journals examined regularly. Various musical subjects included.

0208. Bobillier, Marie. "Bibliographie des bibliographies musicales." *L'Année Musicale*, 3(1913), 1-152. (Reprint–New York: Da Capo Press, 1971). (Da Capo Press Music Reprint Series). ML113 B66
       Duckles 67–1320; Duckles 74–1836; ARBA 72-1089
       The original journal article was issued under the pseudonym "Michel Brenet." It lists some 1,800 items, illustrating the broadest definition of the expression "bibliography": lists of compositions, lists of books, thematic indexes, separately published lists, lists in journals and in books, library and exhibition catalogs, general lists and lists related to individual musicians and particular cities. Unfortunately, it lacks indication of sources consulted, and there is no index.

0209   "Current Catalogues from the Music World," in *Notes; the Quarterly Journal of the Music Library Association*. 2d series. 1943– . (quarterly).
       This useful feature of *Notes* was dropped after the September 1970 issue. It had listed current sales catalogs of dealers (with indicators of topics included), and also of publishers, recording manufacturers, and recording dealers.

0210   Pruett, James. **A Checklist of Music Bibliographies and Indexes in Progress and Unpublished**. 2d ed. Ann Arbor: Music Library Association, 1969. (1st ed. 1963). 25p. (MLA Index Series, 3).
       Duckles 74–1903
       Author list of 150 items, with subject index. Covers lists of writings and lists of musical works.

Many works in subsequent chapters also contain bibliographies of bibliographies.

SELECTIVE AND CRITICAL GUIDES

These are subjective compilations of the "best" or most significant writings within large musical realms.

0211   Aber, Adolf. **Handbuch der Musikliteratur in systematisch-chronologischer Anordnung.** Leipzig: Breitkopf & Härtel, 1922. xx p., 696 columns. (Kleine Handbücher der Musikgeschichte nach Gattungen, 13). (Reprint–Hildesheim: Georg Olms; Wiesbaden: Breitkopf & Härtel, 1967). ML113 A2
    Duckles 67–411; Duckles 74–533
Also cited under 0099. An international bibliography (leaning on German) of books and articles in classified arrangement. Some 13,000 entries. No annotations. Author and subject indexes.

0212   Adlung, Jakob. **Anleitung zur musikalischen Gelahrtheit** . . . 2. Aufl. besorgt von Johann Adam Hiller. Dresden und Leipzig: Breitkopf, 1783. (1st ed. 1758). (Reprint of 1st ed., Faksimile-Nachdruck hrsg. von Hans Joachim Moser–Kassel: Bärenreiter-Verlag, 1953. 814p.). ML100 A2
    Duckles 67–412; Duckles 74–534
One of the earliest critical bibliographies in music; comprised of a series of bibliographic essays on antiquity, singing, tablatures, etc., with the largest section dealing with the organ. Name and subject indexes.

0213   Bryant, Eric Thomas. **Music.** London: Clive Bingley, 1965. 84p. (Readers Guide Series). ML113 B9
Concise introduction to music literature in readable style. Considers reference books, histories, books on vocal and instrumental music, theory, appreciation, and recordings. Author, title, and subject indexes. About 250 annotated entries, mostly in English.

0214   Davies, J. H. **Musicalia: Sources of Information in Music.** 2d ed. Oxford, New York: Pergamon Press, 1969. (1st ed. 1966). xii, 184p. (The Commonwealth and International Library. Libraries and Technical Information Division). ML113 D383 M9
    Duckles 67–1382 (for 1st ed.); Duckles 74–1849
A valuable survey of major sources, arranged according to reader approach (conductor, singer, musicologist, record collector, etc.). Well-selected materials, mostly in English. Illustrated by 48 facsimiles from works discussed.

0215   Duckles, Vincent. "Music Literature, Music and Sound Recordings," in *Bibliography: Current State and Future Trends*, ed. R. B. Downs and F. B. Jenkins (Urbana: University of Illinois Press, 1967), pp.158-85. Z1002 D62
        Duckles 74–1875
        A fine review of recent reference/bibliographic publication in music, covering 113 items. First appeared in *Library Trends*, Jan./Apr. 1967. An index of titles has been added to the book version.

0216   Duckles, Vincent. **Music Reference and Research Materials: An Annotated Bibliography**. 3d ed. New York: Free Press, 1974. (1st ed. 1964). xvi, 526p. ML113 D83
        Duckles 74–1876; Winchell 67–2BH2
        Excellent survey of 1,922 items, grouped primarily by form (dictionaries, histories, yearbooks, etc.), with some topical sections. Concentrates on music and languages of Western Europe and North America, emphasizing serious music. Refers to reviews. Especially good chapter on catalogs of music libraries. Author, title, and subject indexes.

0217   Forkel, Johann Nikolaus. **Allgemeine Litteratur der Musik oder Anleitung zur Kenntniss musikalischer Bücher** . . . Leipzig: Schwickert, 1792. xxiv, 540p. (Reprint–Hildesheim: Georg Olms, 1962). ML105 F73
        Duckles 67–425; Duckles 74–549
        The first attempt at a comprehensive bibliography of music, by a man who has been praised as the founder of musicology. Greater scope and inclusiveness than Adlung (0212), which went before. About 3,000 books are entered, with bibliographic data, citations to literature about the item, and Forkel's comments. Arrangement is by subject, with indexes to authors and anonymous titles. Also a list of manuscripts (books on music) with locations.

0218   Gleason, Harold. **Music Literature Outlines**. 2d ed. Rochester: Levis Music Stores, 1954-58. ML161 G52
        Duckles 67–324; Duckles 74–407
        Five series, as follows: 1, Music in the middle ages and renaissance; 2, Music in the baroque; 3, American music from 1620 to 1920; 4, Contemporary American music; 5, Chamber music from Haydn to Ravel. Summaries of historical development, with extensive reading lists of books and articles.

0219   Haydon, Glen. **Introduction to Musicology: A Survey of the Fields, Systematic and Historical, of Musical Knowledge and Research**. New York: Prentice-Hall, 1941. 329p. ML3797 H29 I6
        Duckles 67–400; Duckles 74–517
        Surveys of the state of knowledge in various musicological areas (theory, acoustics, history of music, pedagogy, etc.) with strong bibliographies. Best review of its kind. For somewhat more recent coverage, an uneven work by Karl Fellerer may be consulted: *Einführung in die Musikwissenschaft* (2. neubearb. und erweiterte Aufl.; Münchberg: B. Hahnefeld, 1953).

0220   Kahl, Willi, and Wilhelm-Martin Luther. **Repertorium der Musik-wissenschaft: Musikschrifttum, Denkmäler und Gesamtausgaben in Auswahl (1800-1950)** . . . Kassel und Basel: Bärenreiter Verlag, 1953. vi, 271p.

Duckles 67–428; Duckles 74–551

An international, classified list of 2,795 numbered items with their locations in German libraries. Periodical articles not placed among the subject lists, but some dissertations are included. A separate list of journals; name and subject indexes. A good basic library of music research writing in Western European languages, slanting toward German. The inventories of historical and collected editions of music (Denkmäler und Gesamtausgaben), however, are less reliable.

0221   Lichtenthal, Pietro. **Dizionario e bibliografia della musica**. Milano: A. Fontana, 1826. 4v. ML100 L69

Duckles 67–432; Duckles 74–294

Volumes 3 and 4 are of principal interest: they are based on a translation into Italian and an update of Forkel (0218) extending to 1826. The first two volumes are a dictionary of terms.

0222   National Association of Schools of Music. **A List of Books on Music.** Memphis, Tenn.: the Association, 1953. 57p. Supplements 1-10, 1936-57. ML27 U5 N25

Duckles 67–466; Duckles 74–602

Intended as a basic buying guide for music schools. Nearly all entries are in English. Comments included. Some selection of musical scores as well. A subject index to the original list and first seven supplements appeared in the NASM *Bulletin*, 33(1952). No supplements published after 1957.

0223   Reese, Gustave. **Fourscore Classics of Music Literature**. New York: Liberal Arts Press, 1957. 91p. (Reprint–New York: Da Capo Press, 1970). (Da Capo Press Music Reprint Series). ML160 R33

Duckles 67–601; Duckles 74–534; ARBA 71–1244

Summaries, a page or so in length, of 80 major writings from antiquity to recent times. The author endeavored to cover important works that had not been translated into English. Authority of the compiler, who is one of the great living musicologists, gives special value to these comments and abstracts. Sequence is chronological; title index.

0224   Rosner, Helmut. **Nachdruck-Verzeichnis der Musikschriftums**. Wilhelmshaven: Heinrichshofen, 1970. 144p. (Taschenbücher zur Musikwissenschaft, 5). ML113 R54

Duckles 74–561

An index to modern reprints of treatises on music; about 1,500 items. No musical compositions covered. Also serves as a foundation list of important theoretical and historical writing.

0225   Watanabe, Ruth T. **Introduction to Music Research**. Englewood Cliffs, N.J.: Prentice-Hall, Inc., 1967. viii, 237p. ML3797 W37

Duckles 74—531; Winchell 67—2BH3

Described in preface as a "practical handbook treating the basic procedures and tools of investigative studies," this is the best modern bibliographic essay that surveys the past and present of music reference. Particularly useful chapters on lists of dissertations and on contemporary music journals. Nearly all entries are English, German, or French. Author, title, and subject indexes.

GENERAL LISTS AND LIBRARY CATALOGS

While the preceding items, 0211 to 0225, offer a selective guidance through the immensity of musical literature, those that follow are comprehensive lists. Most of them set forth the holdings of certain libraries. Similar sources appear in the succeeding section ("Lists of Writings by Historical Period"), but with some kind of historical limitation.

The printed catalog of a large research library is a prism that reflects information of many hues. Any such catalog will give facts of publication ("imprint data"). Many also give descriptions, or at least indications—through subject headings—of the contents of each book. A particularly useful angle of reflection is subject arrangement of the entries, by which we can observe like materials in affinity groups; this aspect—subject arrangement—has been used as a criterion for selecting the works that appear in this section. In all these works it is possible to locate clusters of writings on "music" or diverse related topics. (Some important library catalogs without subject access will be cited at the end of the section.)

One major limitation of such catalogs is that ordinarily they list only "separates"; i.e., books, monographs, dissertations, reports, or whatever—which have been published individually. This means the exclusion of journal articles or essays in collections, even though such formats often contribute depth and vitality within a subject field. (Contrast with unrestricted subject lists, like 0211.)

Critical comment is also missing in library catalogs. And so are indexes; though cross references do some of their work.

0226   Azhderian, Helen Wentworth. **Reference Works in Music and Music Literature in Five Libraries of Los Angeles County**. Los Angeles: Published for the Southern California Chapter of the Music Library Association, by the University of Southern California, 1953. x, 313p. ML113 A94

Duckles 67—413; Duckles 74—535

A "union" (combined) catalog of the Henry E. Huntington Library, William Andrews Clark Memorial Library, Los Angeles Public Library, University of Southern California Library, and University of California at Los Angeles. Total of 4,563 numbered entries in classified order. Includes all titles located in "bibliography" and all titles of periodicals/serials (336 items). Other categories treated more selectively, emphasizing foreign and unusual books. Full imprint data; no commentaries; author index.

Coverage extends beyond "reference" books into all sorts of scholarly material; indeed, the compilation may be used—like 0211 and 0220—for an overview of significant research.

0227 Barcelona (Province). Diputación Provincial. Biblioteca Central. **Catalech de la biblioteca musical** . . . Per en Felipe Pedrell. Barcelona: Palau de la Diputacio, 1908-1909. 2v. ML136 B24

Duckles 67–823; Duckles 74–1148

Includes books and actual music: 1,271 entries in classified arrangement. Richest in Spanish material, but collection touches all of Europe. Most useful for details offered: content descriptions, musical examples, facsimiles, collations and bibliographic notes. Personal name index.

0228 Boston. Public Library. **Dictionary Catalog of the Music Collection.** Boston: G. K. Hall, 1972. 20v. ML136 B7 B73

Duckles 74–1185; ARBA 73–1021

One of the numerous printed versions of library card catalogs that have been issued by G. K. Hall. In the Hall format, actual cards are spread out and photographed just as they are. BPL was a fortunate choice, since its music holdings are outstanding. Some 80,000 entries, including both writings about music and musical scores themselves. The "dictionary catalog" arrangement—found in most American research libraries—mixes subject and author cards in a single alphabet. This publication incorporates the Allen A. Brown Music Collection of BPL, for which an earlier catalog had appeared in 1910-16 (cf. 0373). An extensive collection of sheet music was excluded.

0229 British Museum. Department of Printed Books. **Subject Index of the Modern Works Added to the Library, 1881-1900.** Ed. by G. K. Fortescue. London: the Museum, 1902-1903. 3v. Supplements at approximate five-year intervals; last to appear covers 1956-60 (6v.). Z1035 B865

Winchell 67–AA68

This should be a better key than it is, because the library of the British Museum is one of the three or four greatest in the world. But the *Subject Index* is weak in choice and utilization of headings, and exhibits sundry technical defects that impede use. Nevertheless, it gives some access to more than 900,000 titles, among them a large proportion of European books on music issued in the last nine decades. For subject guide to earlier materials, see 0235. The author catalog of the library is cited at the end of this section.

0230 British Museum. Department of Printed Books. Hirsch Library. **Books in the Hirsch Library, with Supplementary List of Music.** London, Trustees of the British Museum, 1959. 542p. (Catalogue of Printed Books in the British Museum. Accessions, 3rd series, pt. 291B). Z921 B861

Duckles 67–972; Duckles 74–1333

In 1946 the Museum acquired the music library of Paul Hirsch, containing more than 12,000 books in addition to a collection of scores. (A catalog of the original library—books and scores—is cited at 0231. The BM catalog of music in the collection is 0378; the present volume includes a supplement to it.)

0231   Hirsch, Paul. **Katalog der Musikbibliothek Paul Hirsch** ... Hrsg. von
        Kathi Meyer und Paul Hirsch. Berlin, Frankfurt: Breslauer; Cam-
        bridge: Cambridge University Press, 1928-47. 4v. ML133 H64
            Duckles 67—1135; Duckles 74—1559
    This great private library of scores and literature on music was
moved from Frankfurt to England to avoid Nazi confiscation. Its first English
home was Cambridge, where Vol. 4 of the *Katalog* was produced; thence it
moved to the British Museum (cf. 0231). While musical editions draw most
attention, the treatises offer an excellent representation of the history of
music theory.

0232   Milan. Conservatorio di Musica "Giuseppe Verdi." Biblioteca.
        **Catalogo della biblioteca. Letteratura musicale e opere teoriche.
        Parte prima: Manoscritti e stampe fino al 1899**. Milano, Firenze:
        Leo Olschki, 1969. x, 151p. ML136 M6 V5
    Begins a series of catalogs covering the 300,000 volume music
library. This first volume lists 2,458 books on music that were published
before 1900. Author arrangement with subject index. A balanced international collection, strongest in opera and theatre.

0233   New York (City). Public Library. Reference Dept. **Dictionary
        Catalog of the Music Collection**. Boston: G. K. Hall, 1964-65. 33v.
        Supplement, 1966. 811p. Supplement II, 1973. 10v. ML136 N5
        N573
            Duckles 67—1027; Duckles 74—1403
    More than a half million cards were photographed to create this
outstanding repository of information. Covers, in a single alphabetical
arrangement, author entries, subject entries, books, musical scores, and a
great many journal articles. One of the world's great music collections, the
NYPL is strongest in Americana, opera and other vocal music, complete
works and historical editions. With the supplements, library holdings are
recorded into 1972.

0234   Peabody Institute, Baltimore. **Catalogue of the Library**. Baltimore:
        the Institute, 1883-1905. 13v. (Reprint—Boston: G. K. Hall, 1962).
        Z881 B2
            Winchell 67—AA75
    Dictionary catalog of an important collection, now part of the
Enoch Pratt Free Library, Baltimore. Particularly useful for its "analytics":
indexing of parts within larger works. Also gives detailed contents of
multi-volume sets. Subject access is therefore provided for many periodicals
and composite publications that are not presented in other library catalogs
with such minute perspective. Musical scores not included.

0235   Peddie, Robert Alexander. **Subject Index of Books Published before
        1880**. London: Grafton, 1933-48. 4v. Z1035 P37
            Winchell 67—AA61
    Some 200,000 items, alphabetical by subject. Intended as com-
panion work to the British Museum *Subject Index* . . . (0229); together these

two listings offer the most complete compilation of books on music—and other subjects, of course—from the nineteenth century; less reliable for earlier times. Note that Peddie does include books not in the British Museum. Personal name headings are omitted.

0236   U.S. Library of Congress. **Library of Congress Catalog. Books: Subjects** ... Washington: the Library, 1950– . (quarterly; annual and quinquennial cumulations). Z1215 U56
          Winchell 67–AA66
In general limited to monographs and first issues of new periodicals that were published in 1945 or later; but since reprints and revised editions are included for earlier material, the inclusive period is really indefinite in terms of original imprint dates. Entries under all Library of Congress subject headings. Information includes L.C. class numbers, but not "tracings" (other headings used for a work). Few descriptive notes; transliterations for non-Roman scripts often lacking. One must remember that the date of appearance in this catalog will follow by some years the date of the item's publication. This is the most comprehensive source for titles in given subject areas, reflecting the output of all nations, in every language, on every sort of musical topic. Other L.C. catalogs are noted at the end of this section and at 0387.

0237   Warsaw. Uniwersytet. Biblioteka. **Katalog druków muzycznych XVI, XVII i XVIII w** ... Warszawa: Wydawnictwa Uniwersytetu Warszawskiego, 1970– . 379p. (Acta Bibliothecae Universitatis Varsoviensis, 7). ML136 W372 U53
          Duckles 74–1529
Classified inventory of scores and treatises, dating from the sixteenth to eighteenth centuries, in the University of Warsaw. About 1,700 items, mostly from southern and western Europe, thoroughly described with contents of collections, provenance notes, etc. Indexes to composers, anonymous titles, printers (by country/city as well as alphabetically); chronological list of imprints. Commentaries in Polish with summaries in French.

0238   Wolffheim, Werner J., Library. **Versteigerung der Musikbibliothek des Herrn Dr. Werner Wolffheim** ... Berlin: Breslauer & L. Liepmannssohn, 1928-29. 2v. in 4. ML138 W652
          Duckles 67–1138; Duckles 74–1563
Sale catalog of an important private library, consisting of books, manuscripts, and printed scores. Detailed bibliographic descriptions; 89 plates. Classified arrangement of the 4,032 numbered items.

In this section we have taken note of major international compilations of titles with subject access. The search for information on music will usually benefit from an arrangement of entries which brings material together by subject. However, some types of information requirement can be satisfied through lists and catalogs arranged by author: e.g., the need for imprint data on a given work, or the need for titles written by a given scholar. For such facts, the most promising source is "N.U.C.," probably the world's biggest publication.

0239　**National Union Catalog: A Cumulative Author List.** Washington: Library of Congress, 1953– . (monthly, with quarterly and annual cumulations). Z1215 U55
　　　Winchell 67–AA65

More than 750 research libraries cooperate with the Library of Congress in providing titles and cataloging copy for this combined creation. All major alphabets and virtually all languages are represented, with formats including books, pamphlets, reports, maps, atlases, and first issues of new periodicals–but not music scores, which are separately accounted for in 0387. N.U.C. is a successor to author catalogs issued by the Library of Congress in 1942-46 (167v.), 1948 (42v.), 1953 (24v.); those catalogs covered books for which cards had been prepared in the Library from 1898 on. Now in progress is a retrospective element of N.U.C. which will supersede the earlier L.C. author catalogs, and give one-place access to a good share of what has been published in the world:

0240　**National Union Catalog: Pre-1956 Imprints.** London: Mansell, 1968– . (in progress). Z1215 U47
　　　Winchell 67–2AA12

Scheduled for completion around 1978, in 610 volumes. Replaces the L.C. author catalogs cited in 0239 and also that segment of N.U.C. which covered 1953-57 (because contents of that set were repeated in the N.U.C. 1958-62). Will "encompass some 10 million entries and to indicate locations in more than 700 libraries," according to Winchell. Same formats as 0239, but with addition of musical scores, which are listed under composers.

Two other great libraries have issued mammoth catalogs and are keeping them up to date with supplements:

0241　British Museum. Department of Printed Books. **General Catalogue of Printed Books.** London: Trustees of the British Museum, 1931-66. 263v. Supplement, 1956-65. London, 1968. 50v. Z2001 B743
　　　Winchell 67–AA67; 2AA13

Not to be confused with the superseded *Catalogue of Printed Books* prepared at the turn of the century. Basically this is an author catalog, but some forms of subject access are found; e.g., under personal name entries some biographical material may be listed; under countries some works about the country. With more than 4,000,000 entries in 133,000 pages, this inventory of books, periodical titles, and newspapers is an invaluable resource. A large proportion of entries do not appear in the L.C. author catalogs. Cutoff date 1955, which is where the decennial supplements take over. Annual volumes of "additions" also published.

0242　Paris. Bibliothèque Nationale. **Catalogue général des livres imprimés: Auteurs.** Paris: Imprimerie Nationale, 1900– . Z2161 P3
　　　Winchell 67–AA72; 1AA15; 2AA15; 3AA12

Because of the long time span of publication, and the fact that each volume—through volume 188—covered what was in the library at its place in time, this huge compendium is by no means a complete inventory. Beginning with volume 189, only works published before 1960 are included, and all later publications are appearing in the supplement: *Catalogue général des livres imprimés: Auteurs, collectivité–auteurs, anonymes, 1960-64* (Paris, 1965–). Adds 300,000 entries to the main set. Formats covered comparable to those in 0241, with similar inclusion of certain subject approaches.

Another significant set of catalogs should be cited, although its high purchase price has prevented nearly all libraries from buying it:

0243   California. University Library. **Author-Title Catalog** (Berkeley Campus). Boston: G. K. Hall, 1963. 115v. **Dictionary Catalog of the Library** (Los Angeles Campus). Boston: G. K. Hall, 1964. 129v. **University of California Union Catalog of Monographs Cataloged by the Nine Campuses from 1963 through 1967.** Boston: G. K. Hall, 1973. 47v.

A huge inventory; e.g., the Berkeley base set indexed some 2,800,000 items, including title entries for 36,000 serials, and the 1973 supplement contains a million subject entries with 1.6 million author-title entries. Music scores and recordings excluded.

Various other library catalogs may be located through Winchell.

LISTS OF WRITINGS BY HISTORICAL PERIOD

Here we have a number of listings that are international in scope but restricted in time-frame, most often to publications prior to 1800. The first two citations are general, the others exclusively musical.

0244   Brunet, Jacques Charles. **Manuel du libraire et de l'amateur de livres.** 5. éd. . . . Paris: Didot, 1860-80. 9v. (Reprints—Berlin: Altmann, 1921-22, 6v.; Paris: Dorbon-Aini, 1928, 6v.). Z1011 B9 M5
         Winchell 67—AA58
A universal bibliography of significant books, primarily before the nineteenth century and particularly strong in French authors. Bibliographical and critical comments. Advantage over other such endeavors is inclusion of a subject index; base arrangement is by author.

0245   Grässe, Johann Georg Theodor. **Trésor de livres rares et précieux.** Dresden: Kuntze, 1859-69. 7v. (Reprints—Paris: Welter, 1900-1901, iv.; Berlin: Altmann, 1922, 7v.) Z1011 G73
         Winchell 67—AA60
Similar in approach to 0244, with more German inclusions. Lacks the subject index.

Another universal list was cited earlier because of its wider time base: 0235. The items that follow are concerned only with music literature.

0246   Associazione dei Musicologi Italiani. **Catalogo generale delle opere musicali, teoriche o pratiche, manoscritti o stampate, di autori vissuti sino ai primi decenni del XIX secolo, esistenti nelle biblioteche e negli archivi d'Italia.** Parma: 1911– . (in progress; publisher varies). ML136 I8 A8
     Duckles 67–923/941; Duckles 74–1277
A group of catalogs for individual cities (Parma, Bologna, Milano, Firenze, Pistoia, Roma, Venezia, Vicenza, Genova, Modena, Ferrara, Napoli, Assisi, Torino, Pisa, Verona), in which significant holdings of each locale are described. Emphasis on musical manuscripts and editions, but covers also treatises–which are well treated, with tables of contents, etc. Most entries are Italian in origin.

0247   Becker, Carl. **Systematisch-chronologische Darstellung der musikalischen Literatur von der frühesten bis auf die neueste Zeit . . .** Leipzig: R. Friese, 1836. 571 cols., 34 p. Nachtrag, 1839. (Reprint–Hilversum: Frits A. M. Knuf, 1966). Z6811 B391
     Duckles 67–414; Duckles 74–536
Classified bibliography of books and periodical articles on a large number of topics: theory, instruments, individual composers, etc., etc. Detailed descriptions of key works, with some abstracts. Critical comments by Becker, or others (documented); and biographical notes on authors. Among types of literature included are novels and stories about musicians, satires and lampoons. Author/subject indexes; *Anhang* chronology of vocal music collections, 1502-1799. 0421 is a companion work by Becker. Later coverage in 0278 and 0279.

0248   British Museum. Department of Printed Books. **Catalogue of Printed Music Published between 1487 and 1800 Now in the British Museum.** By W. Barclay Squire. London: Trustees, 1912. 2v. First supplement bound in. Second supplement, by W. C. Smith. Cambridge: Cambridge University Press, 1940. 85p. (Reprint–Nendeln, Liechtenstein: Kraus, 1968). ML136 L8 B74
     Duckles 67–970; Duckles 74–1331
Entered here because it does contain books about music. An international group, but strongest in British writers. Some music printed in magazines is included. (See also 0424, 0426.)

0249   Davidsson, Åke. **Bibliographie der musiktheoretischen Drucke des 16. Jahrhunderts.** Baden-Baden: Verlag Heitz GmbH, 1962. 99p. (Bibliotheca Bibliographica Aureliana, 9). ML114 D38
     Duckles 67–597; Duckles 74–776
Very useful list of some 600 treatises, in author sequence. Abundant references to library locations (76 institutions in Europe and the United States) and citations in other bibliographies. No commentaries, however, and

unfortunately no allusions to translations, modern reprints, or critical secondary literature. There are 25 facsimiles.

0250   Davidsson, Åke. **Catalogue critique et descriptif des ouvrages théoriques sur la musique imprimés au XVIe et au XVIIe siècles et conservés dans les bibliothèques suédoises.** Upsala: Almquist & Wiksells, 1953. 83p. (Studia Musicologica Upsaliensia, 2). ML128 T5 D3
    Duckles 67–598; Duckles 74–777
    Descriptive list of 108 items with locations in Swedish libraries. Literature citations given.

0251   The Hague. Gemeentemuseum. **Catalogus van de muziekbibliotheek. Deel I: Historische en theoretische werken tot 1800.** By Marie H. Charbon. Amsterdam: Frits Knuf; New York: Da Capo Press, 1969. 183p. (Da Capo Press Music Reprint Series). ML136 H25 G56
    About 1,200 titles on music history and theory; plus some 90 publishers' catalogs issued prior to 1800. Some useful comments and descriptions, but uneven indexing. Much of this rich collection comes from the library of musicologist Daniel Scheurleer. English summaries of Dutch text.

0252   Mandyczewski, Eusebius. "Bücher und Schriften über Musik. Druckwerke und Handschriften aus der Zeit bis zum Jahre 1800." In *Geschichte der K. K. Gesellschaft der Musikfreunde in Wien* (Wien: Gesellschaft Adolf Holzhausen, 1912, 2v.), pp. 55-84. ML128 V4 G34suppl
    Duckles 67–600; Duckles 74–781
    A strong international list of materials found in the library of the Gesellschaft.

0253   Paris. Bibliothèque Nationale. Département des Imprimés. **Catalogue du fonds de musique ancienne** ... By Jules Écorcheville. Paris: Bibliothèque Nationale, 1910-14. 8v. (Reprint–New York: Da Capo Press, 1972). (Da Capo Press Music Reprint Series). ML136 P2 B44
    Duckles 67–1045; Duckles 74–1427
    Both music and writings about music, issued up to 1750; some 10,000 entries. Includes manuscripts. Author/composer order, with no indexes. See also note following 0414.

0254   Paris. Conservatoire National de Musique   et de Déclamation... **Catalogue bibliographique** ... Par J. B. Weckerlin ... Paris: Firmin Didot et Cie., 1885. xxx, 512p. ML136 P2 C7
    Duckles 67–1047; Duckles 74–1430
    Treatises, plus vocal and instrumental music, up to about 1800; emphasis on French material. Most useful feature is detailed description which is given for theoretical works: each one receives chapter-by-chapter summarization. In the section on musical scores there are also fine descriptions, with examples. Name, genre, and instrument indexes.

0255   Smits van Waesberghe, Joseph. **The Theory of Music from the Carolingian Era up to 1400**. Vol. I. Descriptive Catalogue of Manuscripts. München: G. Henle Verlag, 1961. 155p. (Répertoire International des Sources Musicales, B III-1). ML113 I6
    Duckles 67–603; Duckles 74–780
Most of the *Répertoire Internationale* . . . (generally cited as RISM) is concerned with musical works, so it is fully treated in the next chapter (0419). This volume identifies and describes writings that–in whole or in part–discuss musical matters. Only sources in Latin are considered.

0256   U.S. Library of Congress. **Catalogue of Early Books on Music (before 1800)**. By Julia Gregory and Hazel Bartlett. Washington: Government Printing Office, 1913. 312p. Supplement, 1944. 143p. (Reprint–New York: Da Capo Press, 1969). (Da Capo Press Music Reprint Series). ML136 U5 C3
    Duckles 67–1117; Duckles 74–1532
About 2,000 titles are covered in the base volume plus supplement (both of which are in the Da Capo reprint); they exhibit the L.C. holdings through 1942. The Supplement has a special section of East Asiatic acquisitions–about 50 books. An author list, with full bibliographic detail and cross references.

0257   Wolfenbüttel. Herzog-August-Bibliothek. **Kataloge . . . die neue Reihe. Musik. Ältere Drucke bis etwa 1750**. Hrsg. Wolfgang Schmieder und Gisela Hartwieg. Frankfurt am Main: Klostermann, 1967. 2v. Z929 W623
Includes 337 theoretical works and 56 anonymous literary items, along with 528 single editions of music, 113 music collections and 372 editions of liturgical music. Indexed by year, title, place. See also 0419, Series B, vol. 6.

ANNUAL AND PERIODIC LISTS

Apparently the first systematic attempt to list newly published music and books about music dates from 1817. The bibliographic series which began in that year is still being issued, after more than a century and a half of name changes and format adjustments; the one designation that best identifies the entire set is "Hofmeister"–which is the name of the publisher, and also of one of the editors. This work is of sufficient importance to justify a fairly detailed publishing history.

0258   **Handbuch der musikalischen Literatur**. Hrsg. C. F. Whistling. Leipzig: A. Meysel, 1817. xii, 593p. (Reprint–New York: Vienna House, 1972. 2v.). ML113 H69
    Duckles 67–452; Duckles 74–583
Lists music and books on music which appeared in Germany and her German-speaking neighbors, from about 1790 to September 1816. Material presented in classified arrangement. The first supplement (1818) covered works issued October 1816–September 1817. The second supplement (1819)

covered the period October 1817–April 1819. With the third supplement (1820) the pattern of coverage was established as May-April, and this plan persisted through the tenth supplement (1827). Friedrich Hofmeister edited supplements 2-8; C. F. Whistling numbers 9 and 10.

> **Handbuch der musikalischen Literatur.** 2. Aufl. hrsg. C. F. Whistling. Leipzig: Hofmeister, 1828. 3 supplements, 1829, 1834, 1839. ML113 H71

This revision repeated all entries from the supplements to the first edition—but not from the base volume of the first edition—and added publications through 1828, with a few older works. Coverage of the supplements: first, 1828; second, 1829-33; third, 1834-38. Whistling edited the first; A. Hofmeister the second and third.

> **C. F. Whistling's Handbuch der musikalischen Literatur; oder allgemeines systematisch-geordnetes Verzeichniss der in Deutschland und in den angrenzenden Ländern gedruckten Musikalien auch musikalischen Schriften und Abbildungen** . . . 3. . . . Aufl. . . . hrsg. von Adolph Hofmeister. Leipzig: Friedrich Hofmeister, 1845. 16 supplements, through 1943.

Includes a few publications from Denmark, Netherlands, Sweden, even St. Petersburg; but 99 percent of the contents remain German. Music listed in classified arrangement; books by author. Books included on selective basis, in deference to appearance of Becker's more comprehensive arrays of 1836/1839 (0247). Period covered is 1828-43; i.e., the supplements of the second edition are incorporated.

Supplements to the third edition are confusingly numbered. Because there were three volumes (Bänden) in the 1845 list, the first supplement came out in 1852 as "Band IV," and "Erster Ergänzungsband." The title no longer carried Whistling's name. Coverage: 1844-51. A London publishing house was added to the source list.

"Fünfter Band oder Zweiter Ergänzungsband," 1860; covered 1852-59.

For brevity, succeeding supplements are cited in this form: VI, 3 (for Sechster Band oder Dritter Ergänzungsband):

> VI, 3, 1868. Covers 1860-67.
>
> VII, 4, 1876. Covers 1868-73. Format changed to composer sequence, with classified index.
>
> VIII, 5, 1881. Covers 1874-79. Publisher in Riga added; Low Countries and Scandinavia well represented.
>
> IX, 6, 1887. Covers 1880-85.
>
> X, 7, 1893. Covers 1886-91.
>
> XI, 8, 1900. Covers 1892-97. Title and scope adjusted to encompass "Auslände"; includes, for example, Augener in London.
>
> XII, 9, 1906. Covers 1898-1903.
>
> XIII, 10 [n.d. 1911?] Initiates title and catchword indexing. Title list locates pieces within anthologies (but not all titles

appear under their composers). This, and succeeding volumes, will be very helpful in identifying obscure songs and instrumental pieces of all sorts. Covers 1904-1908.

XIV, 11 [n.d. 1916?] Covers 1909-1913.

XV, 12 [n.d. 1921?] Covers 1914-18.

XVI, 13, 1924. Covers 1919-23.

XVII (title page no longer carries the supplement number), 1929. Covers 1924-28. Includes foreign publications with significant distribution in Germany.

XVIII, 1934. Covers 1929-33. (Reprint, XVII and XVIII—New York: Johnson Reprint Corporation, 1968. 2v.).

XIX, 1943. Covers 1934-40, but only "A–Linke"; ceased publication.

Commencing with the second edition of the *Handbuch*, Hofmeister issued monthly reports of new publications under the name *Musikalisch-literarischer Monatsbericht* (1829-1907); this became *Hofmeisters musikalisch-literarischer Monatsbericht* (1908-1942). With the demise of the *Handbuch*, the series received its current appellation: *Deutsche Musik-bibliographie* (1943–).

The first 23 years of the *Monatsbericht* were cumulated by the *Handbuch*; to shorten the interval between monthly issues and cumulations, the publisher began annual cumulations with 1852, in another work of many titles: *Kurzes Verzeichnis sämmtlicher in Deutschland und den angrenzenden Ländern gedruckter Musikalien* . . . (1852-53); *Verzeichnis der im Jahre . . . erschienen Musikalien* (1854-1928); *Hofmeisters Jahresverzeichnis* (1929-42); *Jahresverzeichnis der deutschen Musikalien und Musikschriften* (1943, v. 92; no issue for 1944; 1945/48, v. 94/97– ; v. 93 was omitted in the numbering). This annual gathering, by whatever name, was cumulated by the *Handbuch* until 1943. (Reprint, v. 1-6, 1852-57—New York: Johnson Reprint Corporation, 1968.)

So the current form of "Hofmeister" is twofold: a monthly *Deutsche Musikbibliographie*, with its cumulated annual *Jahresverzeichnis*. Musical compositions are still listed in classed order, with indexes, and books in author order. Limitation is to publications of Germany, Austria, and Switzerland.

The *Jahrbuch der Musikbibliothek Peters* (0152) presented selective, international lists of books on music (1894-1940). It was succeeded by one of the most comprehensive of the modern annual bibliographies:

0259   **Bibliographie des Musikschriftums.** Leipzig, Frankfurt am Main: Hofmeister, 1936– . (frequency varies; now annual). (Reprint, years 1-4, 1936-39—Millwood, N.Y.; Nendeln, Liechtenstein: Kraus Reprint Company, 1973). ML113 B54
Duckles 67–445; Duckles 74-572

Place and publisher also vary; latest issue seen (covering 1965, published 1972) came from Mainz: Schotts' Söhne. This is an international, subject list of books and periodical articles. Strong in material from non-musical journals and composite books such as Festschriften. Indexes to authors, personal names as subjects, and places; no subject index.

But the outstanding periodic review of new writing in the field of music is of more recent origin:

0260   **Répertoire international de littérature musicale (RILM Abstracts).** Editor-in-Chief Barry S. Brook. New York: International RILM Center, 1967– . (quarterly). ML1 I83
   Duckles 74–584; ARBA 74–1096
   We quote from the prefatory statement in a recent issue: "RILM was established in 1966 by the International Musicological Society and the International Association of Music Libraries to attempt to deal with the explosion in musicological documentation by means of international cooperation and modern technology. It is governed by a *Commission Internationale Mixte* designated by the two founding societies. RILM will eventually be concerned with retrospective materials but is presently concentrating on current literature only. *RILM Abstracts*, the official journal of RILM, publishes abstracts indexed by computer of all significant literature on music that has appeared since 1 January 1967. It appears four times a year, the fourth issue being a cumulative index. Included are abstracts of books, articles, essays, reviews, dissertations, catalogues, iconographies, etc. ...." Titles of publications are given in original language, with English translation; abstracts are all in English. Attempts to be comprehensive with regard to scholarly writing, selective for more popular material. Non-musical journals are examined for pertinent articles. Abstracts are written by the original authors when this is practical; otherwise by a team of editors and "area editors"; some are drawn from other published abstract sources. RILM has set and maintained the highest standards in quality, coverage, and format. The only complaint heard against it—that it runs about two years behind, despite computer techniques—is minor in view of the magnitude of the effort involved. A series of *RILM Retrospectives* began in 1972; they are cited elsewhere in the present work (0113, 0347, 0443).

Using 0258, 0259, and 0260, one may view with some understanding the panorama of musical literature over a hundred and fifty years, and one should be able to locate myriad materials on any musical topic. But considering the limitations of coverage in these three great bibliographies (e.g., linguistic in the *Handbuch* series, temporal in RILM), it is clear that other information sources will be needed. Complementing Hofmeister, there are several national, periodic listings of books in which musical writing can be located via subject arrangement; these are British:

0261   **English Catalogue of Books ... Issued ... in Great Britain and Ireland ... 1801–** . London: S. Low, 1864–1901; London: Publishers' Circular, 1906– . (interval varies). (Reprint through v. 16,

1948-51–Millwood, N.Y.; Nendeln, Liechtenstein: Kraus Reprint Company, 1963). Z2001 E53

Winchell 67–AA505

A "trade list" (including only books on sale by established publishers) for the United Kingdom. Base volume, issued 1914, covered 1801-1836; the next one–numbered as Volume I–covered 1835-63. Later publication at variable intervals, settling into a pattern of five-year volumes in the 1930s and '40s, then reducing the interval to three years (1960-62–).

From 1837-89, subject entries had their own volume, but otherwise the policy has been to use "catchwords"–titles inverted to put key terms together alphabetically–either in the same sequence with authors and regular titles or, more recently, in separate sections.

Like Hofmeister, the ECB is a cumulation of short book lists issued at frequent intervals: the *Publishers' Circular* (1837-1959) and its successor *British Books* (1959–), the former a weekly, the latter monthly. Annual volumes are now being compiled in addition to the permanent three-year cumulations.

0262   **British National Bibliography**. London: Council of the British National Bibliography, British Museum, 1950– . (weekly; quarterly, annual, quinquennial cumulations). Z2001 B75

Winchell 67–AA507

Classified list of books, and first issues of periodicals, published in Britain. Subject and other indexes in the cumulations. For practical purposes, supersedes 0261. Books about music are included here, and also in a newer specialized record:

0263   **British Catalogue of Music**. London: Council of the British National Bibliography, British Museum, 1957– . (quarterly; annual cumulations). ML120 G7 B7

Duckles 67–462; Duckles 74–598

Classified list of books on music and of music scores published in Britain. Title, composer, arranger indexes.

Some other bibliographies of British material, with subject access, can be found in Winchell. They cover relatively short periods, but are necessary if a complete search for musical items is desired (e.g., Arber's *Term Catalogues*, which surveys 1668-1709; Winchell 67–AA499).

For United States publication, we have a chain of bibliographies. The only ones cited here are those with some kind of subject approach.

0264   Roorbach, Orville Augustus. **Bibliotheca Americana, 1820-61**. New York: Roorbach, 1852-61. 4v. (Reprint–New York: Peter Smith, 1939). Z1215 A3

Winchell 67–AA338

Since Roorbach is without subject arrangement, the following is a necessary key:

0265   Dempsey, Karen. **Music and Books about Music in Roorbach's Bibliotheca Americana, 1820-61**. Unpublished paper, Kent State University, School of Library Science, 1972. V. 1.

The first of two projected volumes; this one spans 1820-52, which is the scope of Roorbach's first volume. It extracts from Roorbach all titles which include actual music and all titles dealing with music, insofar as this could be determined from examination of the Roorbach entries and/or the N.U.C. and other standard sources.

0266   **American Catalogue of Books, 1876-1910**. New York: Publishers' Weekly, 1876-1910. 9v. in 13. (Reprint—New York: Peter Smith, 1941). Z1215 A7
        Winchell 67—AA341

Base volume is a record of U.S. books in print as of 1876 (by author, title, and subject); remaining volumes are supplements.

0267   **Cumulative Book Index: A World List of Books in the English Language**. New York: H. W. Wilson, 1898— . (monthly; annual and other cumulations). Z1215 C8
        Winchell 67—AA342; AA343; AA345

A fairly involved publishing history may be traced through the Winchell annotations, but in its present manifestation—which commenced in the volume for 1928/32—C.B.I. is a dictionary listing of new American books with substantial coverage of English language books from other countries.

0268   **American Book Publishing Record**. New York: Bowker, 1960— . (monthly; annual and quinquennial cumulations). Z1201 A53
        Winchell 67—AA344

Classified list of new American books (now more than 30,000 annually), developed from the author lists in *Publishers' Weekly*.

0269   **Subject Guide to Books in Print**. New York: Bowker, 1957— . (annual). Z1215 P97
        Winchell 67—AA349

To understand this and the preceding item, one needs to observe the larger constellation to which they belong. The basic record of American trade publication is found in *Publishers' Weekly* (1872— ; Winchell 67—AA350), arranged by author. A parallel work, *Publishers' Trade List Annual* (1873— ; Winchell 67—AA347), arranges U.S. books still in print at the end of each year according to publisher—indeed, the P.T.L.A. is simply a gathering of publishers' catalogs. In 1948 a yearly author-title index to books cited in P.T.L.A. began to appear, under the name *Books in Print* (Winchell 67—AA348). Finally, a subject access was provided in 1957, with the *Subject Guide to Books in Print*. This *Subject Guide* arranges the material of B.I.P., or P.T.L.A., according to Library of Congress subject headings. It is important to recognize the distinction between *Subject Guide* and 0268: the former includes American publications in print at the time it goes to press each year (some of those publications are recent, others are old favorites); the latter identifies only new issues of the period covered. To exemplify: the *Harvard Dictionary of Music* (0002) would be found in every annual issue of P.T.L.A., B.I.P., and *Subject Guide*, since its first edition of 1944, because it has always been in print. However, it would be found only twice in *Publishers' Weekly*—once for each edition—and likewise only once in 0268, which was not around to catch the 1944 edition but did list the 1969 second edition. C.B.I. (0267) would also list *Harvard Dictionary* twice, one listing for each edition.

A similar pattern exists for French literature. The major retrospective cumulation is:

0270 **Catalogue général de la librairie française, 1840-1925.** Paris: Lorenz, 1867-1945. 34v. Z2165 C35
Winchell 67—AA470
Usually referred to as "Lorenz." Publisher varies. An author-title list for France, with some coverage of Switzerland and Belgium, containing subject indexes. Bibliographic detail and even some biographical notes. For subject access to earlier French writing, the best source is Brunet (0244).

0271 **Bibliographie de la France** . . . Paris: Cercle de la Librairie, 1811— . (weekly; monthly, annual, and larger cumulations). Z2165 B58
Winchell 67—AA473
A complex work of interlocking parts and varying arrangement, which in essence constitutes a record of French publishing output. Classified arrangement. Of special interest for music research because of its irregular supplement "C" in which scores are listed. Titles of cumulations vary (cf. Winchell 67—AA474, AA475).

A more convenient arrangement of books on music and musical scores that were issued in France—but for a shorter period—is in:

0272 **Bibliographie musicale française.** Paris: Chambre Syndicale du Commerce de Musique, 1874-1920. (Reprint—Scarsdale, N.Y.: Annemarie Schnase, 1968-69). (6 issues per year). ML120 F8 B5
Duckles 74—822
Entire run consists of 192 issues, covering 1872 to January 1920. Books and scores. Title and imprint vary.

In some ways the most useful French list is this one:

0273 **Biblio; Catalogue des ouvrages parus en langue française dans le monde entier** . . . Paris: Service Bibliographique des Messageries Hachette, 1933— . (monthly; annual cumulations). Z2165 B565
Winchell 67—AA472
A thorough dictionary catalog of books issued in France, Canada, Switzerland, and other French-speaking nations. Does not include musical scores.

German publication before 1790 (when 0258 began its coverage) can be searched with two guides:

0274   Heinsius, Wilhelm. **Allgemeines Bücher-Lexikon, oder vollständiges alphabetisches Verzeichnis aller von 1700 bis zu Ende 1892 erschienenen Bücher.** Leipzig: Brockhaus, 1812-94. 19v. (Reprint—Graz: Akademische Druck, 1963). Z2221 H47
        Winchell 67—478
        One aspect of the arrangement is "catchword title," which makes possible location of musical items. Books only; no scores.

0275   Kayser, Christian Gottlob. **Vollständiges Bücher-Lexikon, 1750-1910.** Leipzig: Tauchnitz, 1834-1911. 36v. (Reprint—Graz: Akademische Druck, 1961-62). Z2221 K23
        Winchell 67—AA479
        An author-title list, with subject indexes. Much overlapping with 0274 after 1750, but easier subject access. Books only; no scores.

Various other German bibliographies will be cited in Volume 2 of the present work. Those already mentioned do provide answers to most needs.
        Books on music, and also scores, issued in Italy can be traced with little difficulty over a long period—using only two sources:

0276   **Bollettino delle pubblicazioni italiane ricevute per diritto di stampa, 1866-1957.** Firenze: Biblioteca Nazionale Centrale, 1886-1957. 72v. (monthly; annual indexes). Z2345 F63
        Winchell 67—AA562a
        This classified list is the most complete bibliography of books, and scores, that were produced in Italy. The entire 72-year span of the set has been very usefully merged into a single cumulated alphabet of some 700,000 entries, under the name of *Catalogo unico delle biblioteche italiane* (Nendeln, Liechtenstein: Kraus Reprint, 1968; 41v.) or C.U.B.I.; however, this cumulation is without a subject index.

✓ 0277   **Bibliografia nazionale italiana.** Firenze: Biblioteca Nazionale Centrale, 1958— . (monthly; annual cumulations). Z2341 B5
        Winchell 67—AA565; 1AA63; 2AA72
        Classified; author-title-subject indexes. Annual cumulations in alphabetical author (and "main entry") sequence. Music scores included in supplements.

Items 0258 through 0277 are the major periodic lists of books (and in some cases of scores also) that have seen the light in certain principal languages and countries. They all offer some form of subject approach. In Volume 2 of this work, bibliographic sources for all nations will be presented.
        Certain other guides to current publication, restricted in time or content coverage, will be useful on occasion to supplement further the more comprehensive and ambitious bibliographies. Two works provide continuations to the Becker *Darstellung* (0247):

0278   Eitner, Robert. **Bücherverzeichnis der Musikliteratur aus den Jahren 1839 bis 1846 im Anschluss an Becker und Büchting** . . . Leipzig: Breitkopf & Härtel, 1885. 89p. (Monatshefte für Musikgeschichte. 17. Jhg, Beilage). ML117 E36
        Duckles 67–424; Duckles 74–548
        Covers books issued in various European countries, and some musical collections; occasional annotations.

0279   Büchting, Adolf. **Bibliotheca Musica. Verzeichnis aller in Bezug auf die Musik . . . 1847-66, im deutschen Buchhandel erschienenen Bücher und Zeitschriften** . . . Nordhausen: A. Büchting, 1867-72. 2v. Supplement: Erste Fortsetzung . . . 1867-71. 1872. 48p.
        Duckles 67–421; Duckles 74–545
        Note restriction here to German publications, which were also listed—in shorter cumulations—by the supplements to *Whistling's Handbuch* (0258).

        Attention to the international output of books on music (and in some cases of journal writing also) became a feature of several scholarly periodicals beginning in the late nineteenth century. Principal periodicals carrying such new-book lists are cited here in chronological order.

0280   **Vierteljahrsschrift für Musikwissenschaft**. Leipzig: 1885-94. (quarterly).
        Duckles 67–471; Duckles 74–610
        Lists of scholarly books and also important musical editions; contents of musicological journals; covers European languages.

0281   **Zeitschrift der international Musikgesellschaft**. Leipzig: 1899/1900-1913/14.
        Duckles 67–472; Duckles 74–611
        Books and periodical articles in European languages are listed in most issues.

0282   Music Teachers National Association. **Proceedings**. 1906– . (annual). ML27 U5 M8
        Duckles 67–460; Duckles 74–596
        Selective, annotated, classified book lists of English language materials.

0283   **Musical Quarterly**. New York: G. Schirmer, 1915– . (quarterly). ML1 M725
        Duckles 67–463; Duckles 74–599
        Scholarly books in major languages are listed in each issue.

0284   **Acta musicologica**. 1928– . (title varies). ML5 I6
        Duckles 67–439; Duckles 74–565
        Classified, international lists of serious books appeared from 1930 to 1952, when this feature was dropped.

0285 **Notes; The Quarterly Journal of the Music Library Association.** 2d
series. December 1943– . ML27 U5 M695
Duckles 67–459; Duckles 74–595

Lists of new books in various languages; some bibliographic
annotations. Most comprehensive of these current publication lists; but see
0286.

0286 **Fontes artis musicae.** Paris: International Association of Music
Libraries, 1954– . (three per year)
Duckles 67–451; Duckles 74–582

Lists of new books, arranged by country. Generally not as complete
for Western Europe and North America as 0285, but stronger in coverage of
Eastern Europe and Soviet Union.

Aside from periodicals, a pair of specific lists of new books is being
published:

0287 American Bibliographic Service. **Quarterly Check-List of Musicology** . . . Darien, Conn.: American Bibliographic Service, 1959– .
(quarterly). ML128 M8 Q3
Duckles 67–441; Duckles 74–567

Selective, international list of monographic publications, with full
imprint data and prices. Annual author indexes, but no subject indexing.

0288 **Bibliographia musicologica; A Bibliography of Musical Literature.**
Utrecht: Joachimsthal, 1970– . (annual).
Duckles 74–570

An international gathering of scholarly books, arranged by author,
with index by broad topics. Includes reprints and facsimile editions. First
issue, covering the year 1968, contained 2,170 items. Imprint data and prices.

PERIODICAL INDEXES

Many of the works already described provide some access to the
contents of periodicals: encyclopedias, histories, biographies, some of the
selective guides (Chapter 4, second section), etc. But the items in the present
section concentrate on the material found in journals. Foremost among them
is:

0289 **The Music Index.** Detroit: Information Coordinators, Inc., 1949– .
(monthly; annual cumulations).
Duckles 67–458; Duckles 74–594

An international index which now covers 300 journals, mostly on
serious music, but with a number of pop/rock/country titles included.
Subject-author arrangement. Premiere performances noted under names of
composers. Book reviews cited in one list, which therefore serves as a guide to
recent book publication as well. Obituaries noted only under name of the
deceased, rather than in a group of deaths. Some particularly useful headings:

contests and awards, discography, iconography, organ (geographically sub-divided). Entries for each country are subdivided by city. Foreign language diacritical marks are lacking throughout; another disadvantage is slowness of appearance, though at this writing the gap for monthly issues has been reduced to a year (cumulations run two or three years behind).

Used in conjunction with RILM (0260), *Music Index* appears to meet nearly every need for bibliographic control over contemporary writing. Still, we do find a few other indexes that encompass groups of magazines not searched by either RILM or *Music Index*.

0290 **Music Article Guide**. Philadelphia: Music Article Guide, 1966– . (quarterly; annual cumulative index). Z6813 M88
Duckles 74–593; Winchell 67–2BH12
An author-title-subject index to contents of some 150 periodicals, all American. Considerable duplication with *Music Index*, but does cover also some house organs and journals from the music industry and music education which are not done by MI. Includes brief annotations.

0291 **Zeitschriftendienst Musik**. Berlin: Deutscher Büchereiverband, 1966– . (monthly; annual cumulations).
Winchell 67–2BH13
Subject index to about 50 periodicals, most of them German. Some 3,000 articles cited each year.

0292 Witzenmann, Wolfgang. "Bibliographie der Aufsätze zur Musik in aussermusikalischen italienischen Zeitschriften." *Analecta musico-logica*, 4 (1967)– .
Duckles 74–571
Installments appear periodically in *Analecta*. They list material under name of the journal; with name and subject indexes. Very little duplication with RILM or *Music Index*.

0293 Belknap, Sara Yancey. **Guide to the Musical Arts; An Analytical Index of Articles and Illustrations, 1953-56**. New York: Scarecrow Press, 1957. unpaged. ML113 B37
Duckles 67–415; Duckles 74–537
Indexes some 15,000 articles and 6,000 illustrations found in eleven English language and two non-English journals. Coverage of dance and theatre as well as music. Much overlap with *Music Index*. Useful primarily for its guide to illustrations, which makes up a separate section. Continued by 0294.

0294 Belknap, Sara Yancey. **Guide to the Performing Arts**. New York: Scarecrow Press, 1960– . (annual). ML118 G8
Duckles 67–443; Duckles 74–569
Originated as a supplement to 0293; each volume covers a year and is published about three years after the period encompassed. At this writing latest issue is for the year 1968; it indexes 48 publications in theatre, dance,

music, cinema, radio and TV, magic and circus. Titles not covered in *Music Index* are few and not too central: *Compositeur Canadien, Folk Music Journal, Folklore and Folk Music Archivist, Keyboard Jr., Young Keyboard . . .* Illustrations are well described, but not separately listed as in 0293.

An abundance of information about musicians and musical events is printed in newspapers. For most newspapers, the only means of subject access are local unpublished indexes. However, current published indexes are being issued for a few papers—the most useful being the next two titles:

0295   The Times, London. **Index to the Times**. London: The Times, 1907– . (bimonthly; frequency and cumulations vary). AI21 T46
        Winchell 67–AG37
Earlier issues of *The Times* are covered (briefly and not always accurately) by *Palmer's Index to the Times Newspaper, 1790-1941* (Winchell 67–AG38). In the current *Index*, entries under "Music" are plentiful (1½ columns in the Nov./Dec. 1971 issue). Subdivision by name of performer, by awards, etc.; popular and serious music given attention.

0296   **New York Times Index**. New York: New York Times, 1913– . (semimonthly; annual cumulation; frequency and cumulations vary). AI21 N44
        Winchell 67–AG32
An excellent precis of world events, with most comprehensive attention to the New York scene. Concerts and recitals listed (by performer; debuts given special note; reviews cited); festivals, tours, world opera productions with critical reviews cited, etc. Also a standard source for death notices. Patience required in use of this index, which uses non-standard headings and tight printing; and which cumulates only once a year at this time. Popular and serious music covered.

Items 0260 and 0289-0296 are the essential current guides to writing about music in periodicals. The trouble with them—seeing them as a group—is that they don't go back far enough and sometimes lag well behind the present year. These empty spaces can be filled, only in part, by consultation of works in the following group.

0297   **Readers' Guide to Periodical Literature**. New York: H. W. Wilson, 1900– . (semimonthly; quarterly and annual cumulations; cumulations vary). AI3 R48
        Winchell 67–AF122
Now indexes about 160 general and non-technical U.S. periodicals by author and subject. Number and titles of magazines covered have varied from year to year (beginning with 15 titles). The only specifically musical items in the present list are *American Record Guide, High Fidelity/Musical America, Musical Quarterly*, and *Opera News*. However, earlier volumes have carried indexing of several others, such as *Etude* and *Musician*.
        Of course, articles on musical topics are also found in general magazines, so each issue of RG will display a fair selection of musical material under various headings. Time lag is a month or so behind publication of the

magazines. A useful heading is "Musical comedies, revues, etc." under which reviews of Broadway musicals are given.

0298 **Poole's Index to Periodical Literature, 1802-81.** Rev. ed. Boston: Houghton, 1891. 2v. Supplements, 1882-1907. Boston: Houghton, 1887-1908. 5v. AI3 P7
　　　Winchell 67—AF119

Subject index to American and English periodicals, presenting some 590,000 articles in 479 different journals. Only the magazine *Music* is specifically in the field, but such titles as *Nation, Spectator,* and *Saturday Review* carried many relevant articles.

0299 **Nineteenth Century Readers' Guide to Periodical Literature, 1890-99, with Supplementary Indexing 1900-22** . . . New York: H. W. Wilson, 1944. 2v. AI3 B496
　　　Winchell 67—AF121

An author-subject index to 51 magazines. None of them are music magazines, but there are numerous entries for musical subjects (e.g., three columns of citations under "Opera") mostly from *Atlantic* and *Harpers.*

0300 **Social Sciences and Humanities Index.** New York: H. W. Wilson, 1965— . (quarterly; annual cumulations). AI3 R49
　　　Winchell 67—AF124

Prior to 1965 this work was known as *International Index* (0301). Under the present name it deals with over 200 periodicals, American and British. No specifically musical titles are covered, but musical topics occur in many of the magazines included—which are of a more scholarly and specialized character than those of the *Readers' Guide.* No significant time lag in current issues. In late 1974 this index will be divided into separate indexes, one for social sciences and one for humanities.

0301 **International Index to Periodicals.** New York: H. W. Wilson, 1916-65. (frequency and cumulations vary). AI3 R49
　　　Winchell 67—AF124

The first two volumes were originally entitled *Readers' Guide to Periodical Literature Supplement,* but these were later renamed and fitted with new title pages to match the remainder of the set. In 1965 title was changed again, to *Social Sciences and Humanities Index* (0300). Coverage varied considerably throughout the existence of *International Index;* e.g., around 50 foreign-language items were indexed before World War II, but all were subsequently dropped. Specialized works in education and art were carried at first, then transferred to other H. W. Wilson indexes. Though all issues reveal a fair attention to musical topics, only a few actual music magazines were searched (in 1960, for instance, these were *Music and Letters, Notes, Musical Quarterly,* and *Music Review*).

0302 **Subject Index to Periodicals, 1915-61.** London: Library Association, 1919-62. (annual; except quarterly with annual cumulations 1954-61). Z6956 E5 B74
　　　Winchell 67—AF125

Original title was *Athenaeum Subject Index*; changed in 1919. Not published from 1923 to 1925. Peak coverage was about 500 periodicals, including several foreign-language items though most were British and American. During and shortly after World War II, policy adjusted to include only British journals. In music these were (just before the *Index* ceased publication) *Music and Letters*, *Music Review*, *Musical Times*, *Opera*, and *Organ*. Succeeded by three indexes in special fields: *British Education Index*, *British Technology Index*, and—of importance for music research—the following work:

0303   **British Humanities Index, 1962–** . London: Library Association, 1963– . (quarterly; annual cumulations). Z6956 E5 B75
      Winchell 67—AF126
      This is the strongest general index for the music field, with indexing of (1971) *Composer*, *English Church Music*, *Folk Music Journal*, *Galpin Society Journal*, *Music and Letters*, *Music and Musicians*, *Music Review*, *Musical Opinion*, *Musical Times*, *Opera*, *Organ*, *Royal College of Music Magazine*, *Royal Musical Association Proceedings*, and also the *RMA Research Chronicle*, *Strad*, and *Tempo*. See note at 0302.

0304   **Annual Magazine Subject Index, 1907-49; A Subject Index to a Selected List of American and English Periodicals and Society Publications.** Boston: F. W. Faxon, 1908-1952. 43v. AI3 A56
      Winchell 67—AF129
      Contents of a few music magazines (in 1948: *Etude*, *Musical Courier*, and *Musical Quarterly*) are dealt with in the "dramatic index" section. Many entries from other journals as well, under more than a dozen headings. This work was reissued by Faxon in a cumulated single alphabetical sequence, under the name *Cumulated Magazine Subject Index, 1907-1949* (Boston: G. K. Hall, 1964; 2v.).

0305   **Internationale Bibliographie der Zeitschriftenliteratur aus allen Gebieten des Wissens ... 1963/64–** . Osnabrück: Felix Dietrich, 1965– . AI9 I5
      Winchell 67—AF118
      Originally issued as *Bibliographie der deutschen Zeitschriften-literatur ... 1896-1964* (Leipzig, 1897-1964; 128v.) and *Bibliographie der fremdsprachigen Zeitschriftenliteratur ... 1911-1964* (Leipzig, 1911-64; 71v.); new format includes German and non-German journals. In terms of titles checked, this is undoubtedly the most extensive of indexes: the 1970/71 volume lists 13,000 periodicals that were searched. Specifically musical items have never been as numerous—in the original or combined versions of the index—as this vast array of titles would suggest. Probably about 80 or 90 are covered in that impressive listing of 1970/71, and they nearly all duplicate *Music Index* (0289). Questions of thoroughness in the indexing may be raised also, on the basis of the relatively small number of entries to be found under musical topics. Nevertheless, for the pre-1949 period, IBZ will be needed, especially for German material. See also 0351.

0306   Blom, Eric. **A General Index to Modern Musical Literature in the English Language** ... London: J. Curwen & Sons, 1927. xi, 159p. (Reprint–New York: Da Capo Press, 1970). (Da Capo Press Music Reprint Series). ML118 B6
        Duckles 67–417; Duckles 74–541; ARBA 71–1237
    This rather haphazard collection of references to books and periodical articles (offered as an outcome of an "amusement") is of value because it embraces the years 1915-26, when indexing of music journals was minimal and indexing of books on music was confined to the *Essay and General Literature Index* (0360). Books and articles are covered in one subject alphabet, with additional entries for authors of the books. Periodicals indexed are *British Musician, Chesterian, Music and Letters, Musical Opinion, Musical Times, Musical Quarterly, Proceedings of the Royal Musical Association*, and *Sackbut*. Total number of entries between 4,500 and 5,000 (estimated).

0307   **A Bibliography of Periodical Literature in Musicology and Allied Fields. Numbers 1-2, October 1938–September 1940, with a Record of Graduate Theses Accepted, October 1938–September 1939.** Assembled for the Committee on Musicology of the American Council of Learned Societies by D. H. Daugherty, Leonard Ellinwood, and Richard S. Hill. Washington: American Council of Learned Societies, 1940-43. 135, 150p. (Reprint–New York: Da Capo Press, 1972). (Da Capo Press Music Reprint Series). ML3797 A7 R7
        Duckles 67–446; Duckles 74–573; ARBA 73–1017
    The ACLS issued in 1938 a review of musicological research for the previous six years. The two volumes cited here (reprinted in one volume) take the record to 1940; the War put an end to this fine series, which covered more than 300 European and American journals and presented more than 1,800 citations in classed arrangement with annotations for most of them.

0308   Pan American Union. Columbus Memorial Library. **Index to Latin American Periodical Literature, 1929-1960.** Boston: G. K. Hall, 1962. 8v. Z1601 P16
        Winchell 67–AF156
    Selective subject access to some 3,000 different magazines, which yielded 250,000 entries. About 800 entries under the principal music heading; others under related topics such as opera, guitar. Continued by 0309.

0309   **Índice general de publicaciones periódicas latino-americanas. Humanidades y ciencias sociales.** v.1– . 1961– . Boston: G. K. Hall, 1962– . (quarterly; annual cumulations). Z1605 I55
        Winchell 67–AF154
    Continues 0308, with selective subject indexing of some 300 periodicals, of which only a few are musical–and duplicated in *Music Index* (0289). Useful for articles in non-musical journals, primarily on folk music.

Some helpful indexing of journals has appeared in the form of regular features in certain periodicals; examples already cited are 0280 and 0281. Here is another:

0310   **Zeitschrift für Musikwissenschaft.** Leipzig: 1918-35.
        Duckles 67—473; Duckles 74—612
        Includes annual index to some 200 journals. Coverage began with the years 1914-18 in the 1918 index, so this item acts as continuation of 0281. Scope is international.

A number of guides to articles on music found in non-musical journals have appeared. Those concerned only with journals of one country are cited in Volume 2 of this work; two useful international lists are mentioned here:

0311   Refardt, Edgar. **Verzeichnis der Aufsätze zur Musik in den nicht-musikalischen Zeitschriften der Universitätsbibliothek Basel.** Leipzig: Breitkopf & Härtel, 1925. vii, 105p. ML136 B29 U69
        Duckles 67—436; Duckles 74—560
        Some 5,000 entries, in subject array, for articles on music in about 500 general periodicals from various countries, with emphasis on German language publications. Locates much material not caught by other indexes.

0312   "Articles Concerning Music in Non-Musical Journals, 1949-64."
        Current Musicology, Spring 1965, pp. 121-27; Fall 1965, pp. 221-26; Spring 1966, pp. 97-99. ML1 C98
        Duckles 67—442; Duckles 74—568
        Final installment signed by Susan Thiemann. All entries are taken from *International Index*; rearranged under broad musical headings. Citations to book reviews included.

Lists of articles on special topics are common; they are cited in Volume 3 of the present work. One of them is mentioned at this point, however, because its topic is sufficiently general to encompass many subdivisions.

0313   Krohn, Ernst C. **The History of Music; An Index to the Literature Available in a Selected Group of Musicological Publications.** St. Louis: Washington University, 1952. xxi, 463p. (Washington University Library Studies, 3). (Reprint—St. Louis: Baton Music Co., 1958). ML113 K77
        Duckles 67—429; Duckles 74—552
        Subject arrangement (with author index) of material dealing with different aspects of music history which were located in 39 journals through January 1952. Journals covered are standard German and English titles, with a pair in French. Book review citations included.

The following works are valuable when it is necessary to find out which of the periodical indexes covered a given title at a certain time period:

0314   Toy, Jacquelyn. **Indexing of German and English Music Periodicals before 1949**. Unpublished paper, Kent State University, School of Library Science, 1969. 21p.

Shows which index carried coverage of 32 English language and 66 German language journals from 1802 to 1949 connecting with the onset of the *Music Index* (0289). Eleven different indexes are cited.

0315   Marconi, Joseph. **Indexed Periodicals**. Ann Arbor: Pierian Press (in preparation).

Another point of access to the content of journals is through indexes that cover a single title only, usually for a long period. A guide to such indexes is:

0316   Haskell, D. C. **A Checklist of Cumulative Indexes to Individual Periodicals in the New York Public Library**. New York: New York Public Library, 1942.

Includes 6,000 entries, arranged by periodical title. Limited to indexes of complete runs, or at least three volumes of a run. At the alphabetical point "Music . . ." these appear, with their indexes cited: *Music Educators National Conference Yearbooks, Music and Letters, Musical Antiquary, Muzyka* (Warsaw), and *Proceedings of the Royal Musical Association*. Other musical titles scattered.

Some recent individual indexing is noted here:

0317   *Acta musicologica.*
        Adkins, Cecil, and Alis Dickinson. **An Index to Acta musicologica, Vols. 1-39.** (Unpublished typescript).
          Duckles 74–565
        Cited in 0210. Author/subject index, English headings.

0318   *Journal of Aesthetics and Art Criticism.*
        Ciurczak, Peter Louis. **The Journal of Aesthetics and Art Criticism, 1941-64 . . . An Index of Articles and Book Reviews Pertaining to Music . . .** Emporia: Kansas State Teachers College, 1965.

0319   *Journal of the American Musicological Society.*
        Franklin, Carole. **Subject Author Index to the Journal of the American Musicological Society, 1948-66.** Unpublished paper, Kent State University, School of Library Science, 1966. 71p.
        Covers articles only; by author and subject.

0320   *Mededelingenblad.*
        Lagas, R., and Clemens von Gleich. "Systematische inhoudsopgave van het Mededelingenblad, Nrs. 1-26." *Mededelingenblad ver nederlandse musikgeschichte*, 26 (Sept. 1968), 9-22.
        Author-subject index to the entire run, 1961-68 (discontinued publication).

0321   *Music and Letters.*
Blom, Eric, and Jack A. Westrup. **Music and Letters: Index to Volumes I-XL.** London: Oxford University Press, 1962.
Duckles 67—465; Duckles 74—601
Articles and book reviews, by author and subject.

0322   *Musical Quarterly.*
Goodkind, Herbert K. **Cumulative Index to the Musical Quarterly, 1915-59.** New York: Goodkind Indexes, 1960. Supplement, 1960-62. New York: Goodkind Indexes, 1963.
Duckles 67—464; Duckles 74—600
Covers articles, book reviews, and the "Current Chronicle."

0323   *Proceedings of the Royal Musical Association.*
Royal Musical Association. **Index to Papers Read before the Members . . . 1874-1944.** Leeds: Printed by Whitehead & Miller for the Royal Musical Association, 1948. 56p. ML128 L8 M8
Duckles 67—469; Duckles 74—606
Subject-author index.

0324   *La Rassegna musicale.*
Allorto, Riccardo. **Indice generale . . . 1928-52.** Torino: Roggero & Tortia, 1953. 174p.
Duckles 67—467; Duckles 74—604
Articles, book reviews, performance reviews, recording reviews.

0325   Degrada, Francesco. **Indici de la Rassegna musicale (annate XXIII-XXXII, 1953-62) e dei Quaderni della Rassegna musicale (N. 1, 2, 3, 1964-65).** Firenze: Leo S. Olschki, 1968. 83p.
Subject-author index to *Rassegna* and its companion publication.

0326   *Revue de musicologie.*
Index général (1917-66). Paris: Société Française de Musicologie, 1968. 38p.
Author/subject arrangement.

0327   *Rivista musicale italiana.*
Parigi, Luigi. **Indici dei volumi I a XX (1894-1913).** Torino: Fratelli Bocca, 1917. 256p.
Duckles 67—468; Duckles 74—605
Articles and reviews covered.

0328   Salvatori, A., and G. Concina. **Indici dei volumi XXI a XXXV (1914-28).** Torino: Fratelli Bocca, 1931. 195p.
Duckles 67—468
Articles and reviews covered; also a list of musical examples.

0329   Degrada, Francesco. "Indici della Rivista musicale italiana,
        1929-55." *Quaderni* 1 (1966).
        The *Rivista* suspended publication with v. 57-2 (April-June 1955).

0330   *Speculum.*
        Wolff, Arthur Sheldon. **Speculum: An Index of Musically Related
        Articles and Book Reviews.** Ann Arbor: Music Library Association,
        1970. (MLA Index Series, 9).
        Duckles 74–608

Various other journals have published occasional indexes to seg-
ments of their output; e.g., the following (cited in Charles 0391, section D):
Ethnomusicology, v.1-10; *Galpin Society Journal*, v.1-5; *Jahrbuch der
Musikbibliothek Peters*, v. 1-40; *Kirchenmusikalisches Jahrbuch*, v. 1-20;
Monatshefte für Musikgeschichte, 1869-78; *Recherches sur la musique
classique française*, v. 1-5; *La Revue musicale*, v. 1-11; *Vereeniging voor
Nederlands Muziekgeschiedenis. Tijdschrift . . .* , v. 1-19 (cumulative contents
table); and *Vierteljahrsschrift für Musikwissenschaft*, v. 1-10. Note also
listings in Haskell (0316).

Before we leave periodical indexes, it may be in order to put them
into a rough chronological perspective. Suppose we have the task of searching
out journal articles on a given topic, say "Lute." The most recent writing
covered by indexes will be located through *Readers' Guide* (0297), *Social
Sciences and Humanities Index* (0300), *British Humanities Index* (0303),
Zeitschriftendienst Musik (0291), *Music Article Guide* (0290) and possibly
the newspaper indexes (0295, 0296). Older material—a year old, at
least—appears in *Music Index* (0289) and *RILM Abstracts* (0260). Writings
from January 1967 onward will be revealed by RILM, which should cover
everything in *Music Index* plus, of course, non-periodical items and contents
of non-musical journals. Material from 1949 to 1966 should be found in
Music Index. For the period 1936 to 1965 there is good international
coverage of journals and monographs in *Bibliographie des Musikschriftums*
(0259). *Guide to the Musical Arts* would bring out any photos of the lute in
the journals from 1953 to 1956 (0293).
        The decade of the forties (1941 to 1948, actually) is poorly covered;
the best approaches are through IBZ (0305), *Subject Index to Periodicals*
(0302), *Annual Magazine Subject Index* (0304), and *International Index*
(0301). Krohn's *History of Music* (0313) would catch certain material on
historical aspects of the lute. For the brief period of its existence, strong
coverage is offered by the *Bibliography of Periodical Literature . . .* (0307); it
encompasses 1938 to 1940. For the mid-thirties we are dependent on 0301,
0302, 0304, 0305, 0313, but from 1935 back to 1914 there is extra help
from the annual indexes in *Zeitschrift für Musikwissenschaft* (0310). Other
extra helpers appear as we continue backward in the retrospective search:
Refardt's list of articles in non-musical journals (0311), Blom's selective index
(0306) and—for material before 1922—Aber's *Handbuch* (0211). Early
twentieth century articles are given in the annual indexes of *Zeitschrift der*

internationalen Musikgesellschaft (0281); aside from that there is only *Readers' Guide* as a contemporary index for English and IBZ in its *Deutschen Zeitschriftenliteratur* series (0305) for German.

Late nineteenth century articles are listed in *Vierteljahrschrift...* (0280) and *Nineteenth-Century Readers' Guide* (0299). For the rest of the nineteenth century we need to use *Poole's Index* (0298), but access to scholarly research on the lute is not likely to turn up there. Indeed, the only promising sources of journal articles from such distant times are subject essays with appended bibliographies, such as the one in MGG (0058). Of course, individual indexes to specific older journals, such as PRMA (0324) could be checked as a laborious last resort.

DISSERTATIONS AND THESES

More than 15,000 doctoral dissertations are produced annually in the United States alone, and other countries have large and increasing numbers of these studies. Bibliographic control over the genre is diffused: there is no truly international index of dissertations (neither for general nor for special subject approaches), and periodical indexes usually bypass this medium. Listings of monographs, such as the *British National Bibliography* (0262) or *National Union Catalog* (0239) include dissertations only if they are published (BNB) or individually cataloged (NUC)—which leaves most of the dissertations unaccounted for. Research at the lower academic levels, e.g., in the form of a master's thesis, is hardly recorded at all.

What coverage there is in these areas is national in scope, and strictly speaking the relevant bibliographies should all be presented in Volume 2 of the present work. Most of them are indeed listed there, but it appears convenient to offer certain titles here because of their importance on the international plane.

0331　**Dissertation Abstracts International**, v. 1– , 1935– . Ann Arbor: Xerox University Microfilms, 1935– . (monthly; annual cumulations). Z5055 U5 A53

　　　Winchell 67–AI11, 3A12; ARBA 72–572

Title varies: Vols. 1-11 (1935-51): *Microfilm Abstracts*; Vols. 12-29 (1952-68): *Dissertation Abstracts*; present title since Vol. 30, No. 1, July 1969. Summarizes dissertations accepted by some 160 cooperating institutions, mostly American but (beginning 1969) with some European representation. Arranged in large subject categories with author and keyword-in-title indexes in monthly issues with annual cumulations. About 50 to 75 musical papers are included each year. A useful *Retrospective Index* for Vols. 1-29 was published in 1970 (9 v. in 11; music items in Vol. 8; Winchell 67–3A12).

Earlier dissertations, and those issued by universities that do not send information to 0331, may be searched in:

0332   U.S. Library of Congress. Catalog Division. **List of American Doctoral Dissertations Printed in 1912-38.** Washington: Government Printing Office, 1913-40. 26v. Z5055 U5 A5
Winchell 67—AI8
Alphabetical and classed lists, with subject index. Restricted to printed dissertations of about 45 institutions. Coverage expanded and continued in the following:

0333   **Doctoral Dissertations Accepted by American Universities, 1933/34–1954/55.** Compiled for the Association of Research Libraries. New York: H. W. Wilson, 1934-56. Z5055 U5 A52
Winchell 67—AI9
Ceased publication with No. 22, covering 1954/55. Included Canadian works. Subject order, author index. Continued by the following:

0334   **Index to American Doctoral Dissertations, 1955/56–** . Compiled for the Association of Research Libraries. Ann Arbor: Xerox University Microfilms, 1957– . (annual).
Winchell 67—AI10
Appears as No. 13 of *Dissertation Abstracts International* (0331). Covers Canada and the United States, with comprehensive lists of more than 15,000 items annually. Subject arrangement, author index.

A vast cumulation of titles, virtually replacing items 0332, 0333, and 0334 (which are still useful for their chronological perspectives) is now available:

0335   **Comprehensive Dissertation Index, 1861-1972.** Ann Arbor: Xerox University Microfilms, 1973. 37v.
Attempts to list all U.S. dissertations, beginning with Yale's three doctorates of 1861; also some foreign coverage. Total of 417,000 titles. Detailed subject arrangement, author indexes. Music entries cover pages 269-589 of Vol. 31, an estimated 24,000 entries. Supplements are planned.

Some earlier international coverage was available through:

0336   Paris. Bibliothèque Nationale. Département des Imprimés. **Catalogue des dissertations et écrits académiques provenant des échanges avec les universités étrangères et reçus par la Bibliothèque Nationale, 1882-1924.** Paris: Klincksieck, 1884-1925. Z5053 P22
Winchell 67—AI7
European universities; arrangement is by university.

Other general listings of dissertations may be seen in Winchell (section AI) and Watanabe (0225), Chapter 8. We now turn to specifically musical compilations, presenting here those of widest scope and utility and reserving for Volume 2 most of those with topical or national limits.

0337   Adkins, Cecil. **Doctoral Dissertations in Musicology.** 5th ed. Phila-
        delphia: American Musicological Society, 1971. (Earlier editions:
        1951, 1958, 1961, 1965). 203p. ML128 M8 J6
        Duckles 67–508 (for 4th ed.); Duckles 74–650; ARBA 72-1088
        Editor and publisher vary. Supplements in *Journal of the American
Musicological Society* each year. Although each edition more or less replaces
the one before, not all entries are carried over. Scope changes take place in
each edition, tending in general to limit coverage within more tightly defined
boundaries of "musicology"; as a result many titles in music education,
psychology of music, and other interdisciplinary fields are being dropped. A
thorough search, therefore, requires attention to the whole set of editions
plus the annual supplements in JAMS. Fifth edition covers 1,917 titles from
56 U.S. and two Canadian universities. Classified arrangement; subject and
author indexes. Dissertations in progress are included. Citations to *Dissertation Abstracts International* (0331) and *RILM Abstracts* (0260) are made
when appropriate.

    Because music education is treated selectively in 0337, specialized
compilations are needed for that area. This series gives good American
coverage:

0338   Music Educators National Conference. Music Education Research
        Council. **Bibliography of Research Studies in Music Education,
        1932-48.** Compiled by William S. Larson. Rev. ed. Chicago: Music
        Educators National Conference, 1949. (1st ed. 1944). 119p. ML120
        U5 M83
        Duckles 67–515; Duckles 74–658
        Some 1,600 items, including master's theses and doctoral disserta-
tions.

0339   Larson, W. S. "Doctoral Dissertations in Music and Music Education,
        1949-56." *Journal of Research in Music Education*, 5 (Fall 1957),
        61-225. ML1 J6
        Duckles 67–512; Duckles 74–658
        This series continues in JRME; a cumulated list for 1957-63
appeared in the Spring 1964 issue, followed by annual lists in Spring. Another
cumulation (1968-71) came out in Spring 1972. Editor varies.

    Another source for American and some European writings:

0340   "Dissertations," in *Current Musicology*, 1965– . (two per year).
        Duckles 67–507; Duckles 74–652
        Lists of completed and in-progress writings; selective basis. Appears
in most issues, under various editors. Two or three new dissertations are
critically reviewed in each issue.

    The newest locator for European research is:

0341   Adkins, Cecil. "Musicological Works in Progress." *Acta musicologica*,
        44 (1972), 146-69.
        Duckles 74—657
        The first annual listing of dissertations and other research in progress
outside North America. A project of the International Center for Musical
Works in Progress, of the International Musicological Society. 178 titles by
authors from 15 countries.

        For master's theses, these sources are important:

0342   **Masters Abstracts: Abstracts of Selected Masters Theses on Micro-
        film.** Ann Arbor: Xerox University Microfilms, 1962— . (quarterly).
        Z5055 U49 M38
        Classified, selective list. About 40 institutions; some 20 musical
items annually.

0343   DeLerma, Dominique René. **A Selective List of Masters' Theses in
        Musicology.** Philadelphia: American Musicological Society, 1970.
        42p. ML128 M8 D4
        Duckles 74—651
        The 257 titles covered were submitted by 36 universities as their
most worthy productions.

0344   "Masters' Theses in Musicology." *Current Musicology*, 12 (Sept.
        1971), 7-37.
        First installment of a projected series. Covers output of American
universities, 1965-70. About 600 titles in subject groups; no author index.

        Some major sources for other countries follow:

0345   "Register of Theses on Music." *Royal Musical Association Research
        Chronicle*, 3 (1963), 4 (1964), 6 (1966), 8 (1970). Compiled by Paul
        Doe.
        Duckles 67—509; Duckles 74—653
        The 1963 list covered the preceding 25 years of British university
output, by subject (265 entries). Supplements, amendments and additions
appear in the later installments. Works in progress are included.

0346   Callaway, Frank. "Register of Theses on Musical Subjects Accepted
        for Higher Degrees and Research Projects on Musical Subjects in
        Progress for Higher Degrees at Australian and New Zealand
        Universities." *Studies in Music*, 1 (1967), 102-107.
        A classified list of 54 accepted works and 26 in progress, for the
period 1927-67.

0347   Gribenski, Jean, *et al.* **French Dissertations in Music: An Annotated
        Bibliography.** New York: RILM Abstracts (in preparation). (RILM
        Retrospectives, 2).

0348   Schaal, Richard. **Verzeichnis deutschsprachiger musikwissenschaft-licher Dissertationen, 1861-1960.** Kassel: Bärenreiter, 1963. 167p. (Musikwissenschaftliche Arbeiten, hrsg. von der Gesellschaft für Musikforschung, 19).
Duckles 67–517; Duckles 74–664
An author list of 2,819 items, with subject index. Supplementary titles given in reviews by Erich Schenk, *Musikforschung*, 17 (1964), 421f.; and Othmar Wessely, *Musikforschung*, 20 (1967), 57-61.

0349   "Dissertationen," in *Musikforschung*, v. 1– . 1948– . ML5 M9437
Duckles 67–511; Duckles 74–656
Periodic lists, with some reviews, of German, Austrian, and Swiss dissertations.

0350   Svenskt Musikhistoriskt Arkiv. **Bulletin**, 1– . 1966– .
Lists of Swedish dissertations and master's theses, completed or in progress, at the Universities of Uppsala, Stockholm, Gothenburg, and Lund.

REVIEWS OF BOOKS

In several of the sources already cited there are references to the locations of book reviews: *RILM Abstracts* (0260), *Music Index* (0289), *History of Music* (0313), etc., etc. But the most convenient review finders are those mentioned in the present section.

0351   **Bibliographie der Rezensionen und Referate, 1900-43.** Leipzig: Dietrich, 1901-1944. v. 1-77. (Internationale Bibliographie der Zeit-schriftenliteratur, Abteilung C). (Reprint–New York: Kraus Reprint Corp., 1962). AI9 B9
Winchell 67–AA313
A section of 0305, which indexed reviews in German and non-German periodicals, some 6,000 different journals at one time or another. Ceased publication during the war, but continues with the following:

Internationale Bibliographie der Rezensionen wissenschaftlicher Literatur. Osnabrück: Dietrich, 1971– . AI9 I55
Some 1,700 journals consulted. Reviews listed by subject (4 columns under "Musik" in the 1971 volume), with author and reviewer indexes.

0352   **Book Review Digest,** 1905– . New York: H. W. Wilson, 1905– . v. 1– . (monthly; semiannual and annual cumulations). Z1219 C96
Winchell 67–AA314
American books which are reviewed in 75 American or British periodicals are subject to inclusion if they receive a certain number of reviews. About 4,000 books covered each year, with at least one citation to a review; most books have more than one citation. Brief description of each book, and quotations from reviews. Author arrangement with subject index and title index; indexes cumulate to five-year intervals.

0353   **Book Review Index**, 1965– . Detroit: Gale Research, 1965– .
        v. 1– . (bimonthly; annual cumulations; frequency varies). Z1035
        A1 B6
            Winchell 67–AA314a; ARBA 71–50
Scanning more than 230 periodicals, BRI editors cover some 65,000
reviews of 35,000 new books every year. After the first three volumes it
suspended publication, but the intervening years before resumption
(1969-72) are being issued. About a half million reviews covered by the series
to date. Arrangement is by author only; no information given about the
book, or the review (except where to find it). Reviews of music in a variety of
periodicals, e.g., *American Record Guide*, *Choice*, *Library Journal*, *Listener*,
Musical Quarterly, and *Notes*.

0354   **Index to Book Reviews in the Humanities**, 1960– . Detroit: Phillip
        Thomson, 1960– . v. 1– . (annual). Z1035 A1 I63
            Winchell 67–AA315; ARBA 71–53
Covers reviews in some 200 English language periodicals, only a third
of which are also indexed by 0353. Author order; no subject approach.
Originally searched for reviews of books in the humanities, but since 1971 has
indexed all reviews in certain humanities periodicals.

0355   New York Times. **New York Times Book Review Index, 1896-1970**.
        New York: Arno Press, 1973. 5v.
Locates reviews that have appeared in the *New York Times* by
author of book, author of review, book title, subject, and category. Almost
800,000 entries in 5,120 pages.

OTHER INDEXES

This is a miscellaneous gathering of important titles, each of which
gives guidance to material in a very specialized category.

0356   Blum, Fred. **Music Monographs in Series: A Bibliography of
        Numbered Monograph Series in the Field of Music Current since
        1945**. New York: Scarecrow Press, 1964. 197p. ML113 B63
            Duckles 67–418; Duckles 74–542
Gives all the titles issued under "series" designations since 1945;
covers 250 series from 30 countries. In series order, with author index. See
also the Charles *Handbook* (0391).

0357   Briquet, Marie. **La Musique dans les congrès internationaux
        (1835-1939)**. Paris: Heugel, 1961. 124p. (Publications de la Société
        Française de Musicologie, 2ème sér., 10).
            Duckles 67–420; Duckles 74–544
Class list of 164 congress proceedings and reports, noting all musical
papers presented. Author, subject, chronological, geographical arrangements.
A heavy European emphasis is found–e.g., there are only two city entries for
New York, but five for Prague and 40 for Paris.

0358   Carl Gregor, Duke of Mecklenburg. **Bibliographie einiger Grenz-gebiete der Musikwissenschaft**. Baden-Baden: Librairie Heitz, 1962. 200p. (Bibliotheca Bibliographica Aureliana, 6). ML128 M8 C4
        Duckles 67–422; Duckles 74–546
Intended to cover writing in disciplines related to music; but many entries are simply about music. Author list of 3,519 items, with subject index in broad headings. Includes books, periodical articles, dissertations. Omissions easy to find: e.g., aesthetics references have no citation to writings of Suzanne Langer.

        Charles, Sydney Robinson. **A Handbook of Music** . . .
        See 0391.

0359   Coover, James. "Music Theory in Translation: A Bibliography." *Journal of Music Theory*, 3 (1959), 70-95. Supplement: 13 (1969), 230-48. ML1 J68
        Duckles 67–596; Duckles 74–775
Alphabetical author list of early theoretical treatises, with reference to translations in various languages. More than 500 entries.

0360   **Essay and General Literature Index, 1900-1933: An Index to About 40,000 Essays and Articles in 2,144 Volumes of Collections of Essays and Miscellaneous Works** . . . New York: H. W. Wilson, 1934. 1952p. Supplements and cumulations as follows: 1934-40, 1941-47, 1948-54, 1955-59, 1960-64, 1965-69; semiannual and annual issues between large cumulations. 70-year index, 1973.
        Winchell 67–BD145
A guide to the contents of composite books, whether by a single author or various authors; author, subject, and some title access. List of books indexed is found in each volume; names of all essays in works by a single author are given—but titles are not listed in multi-author anthologies. Best source for finding critical material of less than book length outside of periodicals: e.g., Huneker's essay on Parsifal is in his 1961 volume *Overtones*. About 200,000 essays covered 1900-1969.

0361   Gerboth, Walter. **An Index to Musical Festschriften and Similar Publications**. New York: W. W. Norton, 1969. ix, 188p. ML128 M8 G4
        Duckles 74–559; Winchell 67–3BH1; ARBA 70–22
A list of *Festschriften* (composite dedicatory volumes), with subject and author indexes of the essays contained in them. Some 3,000 essays in more than 500 volumes are included, up to a 1967 cutoff date.

CHAPTER 5

LISTS OF MUSIC

We now move from writings about music to the compositions themselves. This chapter cites the most important general lists which include titles of musical works. Some are entirely concerned with music, others have relatively little musical coverage; but in each of them certain categories of musical compositions can be located.

Pursuing the principle of earlier chapters, those lists that are completely identified with a particular musical genre—such as opera, or violin music—are reserved for later attention (in Volume 3 of the present work). However, composite bibliographies that subdivide into topical units are included in this chapter—such as the B.B.C. catalogs (0374/77).

BIBLIOGRAPHIES OF LISTS OF MUSIC

There are no comprehensive, or continuing, lists of lists of musical compositions; nothing exists that is comparable to the lists of lists of writings cited earlier (e.g., Besterman, 0206; *Bibliographic Index*, 0207). Partial compilations may be seen in *Harvard Dictionary* (0002, under "Bibliography of Music"), MGG (0058, under "Musikbibliographie"), and Duckles (0216, under "Bibliographies of Music").

This little inventory, cited earlier, may be of some use:

Pruett, James. **Checklist of Music Bibliographies** . . .
See 0210.

SELECTIVE AND CRITICAL LISTS

These titles represent the varied thinking of several musicians regarding basic repertoire, with a diversity of additional information.

0362   Aronowsky, Salomon. **Performing Times of Orchestral Works.** London: E. Benn, 1959. 802p. ML128 O5 A75
        Duckles 67–606; Duckles 74–798
Useful as an overview of principal compositions in many forms, both originally for orchestra and in arrangements. Performing times subjectively derived. Universal, but with British flavor. About 15,000 entries.

0363   Bryant, Eric T. **Music Librarianship: A Practical Guide**. London: James Clarke; New York: Hafner, 1959. xi, 503p. ML111 B83
        Duckles 67–612; Duckles 74–802

Cited here for the long list (pp. 287-487) of musical scores in classed sequence, with annotations. It is a good view of the essential repertoire, but not without British emphasis.

0364   Buschkötter, Wilhelm. **Handbuch der internationalen Konzert-literatur.** Berlin: Walter de Gruyter, 1961. 374p. ML113 B95
        Duckles 67–668; Duckles 74–884
        A very extensive list, arranged chronologically under composers' names, of orchestral music and concertos. Performance time given (without source for it). Interesting for hundreds of obscure works. Uneven in coverage, with Europeans faring better than Americans (e.g., four titles by Zilcher and four by Zillig, but only two by Ives and none by Leonard Bernstein). No title index.

0365   Daniels, David. **Orchestral Music: A Source Book.** Metuchen, N.J.: Scarecrow Press, 1972. 301p.
        Duckles 74–888; ARBA 73–1032
        A list of what the author sees as the active current repertoire of American orchestras, with instrumentation: about 2,500 works in all. Lacks title index, and unfortunately omits diacritical marks on European entries.

0366   Dove, Jack. **Music Libraries, Including a Comprehensive Bibliography of Music Literature and a Select Bibliography of Music Scores Published since 1957** . . . London: Andre Deutsch, 1965. 2v. ML111 M15
        Duckles 67–433; Duckles 74–813
        Based on a work of the same title by Lionel McColvin and Harold Reeves (1937-38), which included a classified list of music. Dove has provided a more recent compilation of representative modern works. British emphasis.

0367   Fuchs, Julius. **Kritik der Tonwerke . . . die Komponisten von Bach bis zur Gegenwart.** Leipzig: Hofmeister, 1897. 400p. (French trans.: *Critique des oeuvres musicales*. Paris: A. Fontemoine, 1900).
        A curious and probably unique attempt to rate composers . . . thousands of them. They are listed in classes of quality: I-1 contains only Bach, Beethoven, Handel and Mozart; I-2 is Schubert; I-3, Gluck and Haydn; II-1 is Brahms, Mendelssohn, Schumann, Wagner, Weber. After that there are large numbers in each class, revealing a fascinating turn-of-the-century value ladder (e.g., in II-2, Chopin, Liszt, and Rossini share the ground with Becker, Bruhns, Goetz, Lotti . . . and also Verdi and Tchaikovsky). Occupants of lower classifications include vast numbers of worthies totally unknown to the present writer, suggesting the immense range of listening engaged in by Mr. Fuchs, and his remarkable capacity for judging what he heard. In a second section, he displays a huge inventory of instrumental pieces (piano, vocal, violin, various combinations, etc.), with gradings of their performing difficulty. Finally there is a composer list of all works cited, with ratings and gradings.

0368   National Interscholastic Music Activities Commission. **Selective Music Lists: Instrumental and Vocal Solos, Instrumental and Vocal Ensembles, Woodwind, Brasswind, String, String-Wind; Boys' Voices, Girls' Voices, Mixed Voices, Madrigal Groups**. Washington: the Commission, 1965 (i.e., 1966). vi, 178p. ML132 A2 N35
Pieces for various solo and ensemble combinations, by grade level and composer order within levels; no comments or indexes.

0369   Reddick, William J. **The Standard Musical Repertoire, with Accurate Timings**. Garden City, N.Y.: Doubleday, 1947. 192p. (Reprint—New York: Greenwood Press, 1969). ML113 R4
    Duckles 67–633; Duckles 74–815
Piano, violin, vocal solos, symphonic works, choral works. Timings taken from recordings, which are identified (often more than one performance for a piece, to give benefit of comparison). Of interest as a good brief repertoire, and also for the comparative timing feature, which offers a cross-section of interpretations by various artists.

GENERAL LISTS AND LIBRARY CATALOGS

Only the most important and extensive general catalogs of libraries are mentioned in this section. Others are cited in Volume 2 (if they have only local materials) or Volume 3 (if they are subject oriented) or in the volumes on individual composers. Bibliographies of library catalogs, in geographical arrangement, appear in *Harvard Dictionary* (0002) and Duckles (0216).

0370   Aarhus, Denmark. Statsbiblioteket. **Fagkataloger** ... 2. forøgede udg. Aarhus: Aarhus Stiftsbogtrykkerie, 1946-57. 4v. Z941 A233
    Duckles 67–817; Duckles 74–1140
Scores take up three volumes; books the other. Music is classed by genres in very detailed breakdowns of instrumental combinations. A strong universal collection. Catalog useful for checking facts on a wide repertoire.

Barcelona (Province) ...
See 0227.

0371   Berlin. Königliche Hausbibliothek. **Katalog der Musiksammlung** ... Leipzig: Breitkopf & Härtel, 1895. x, 356p. ML136 B5 H3
    Duckles 67–840; Duckles 74–1169
A composer list of 6,836 items, strongest in eighteenth and nineteenth century German and Italian works. Non-descriptive.

0372   Bologna. Liceo Musicale. Biblioteca. **Catalogo della biblioteca del Liceo Musicale** ... Compilato da Gaetano Gaspari ... Bologna: Libreria Romagnoli dall' Acqua, 1890-1943. 5v. (Reprint, with corrections—Bologna: Forni, 1961). (Studi e Testi di Musicologia). ML136 B6 L6

Duckles 67–847; Duckles 74–1177

A very strong general collection, arranged by genre with composer index.

0373   Boston. Public Library. **Catalogue of the Allen A. Brown Collection of Music** . . . Boston: the Library, 1908-1916. 4v. ML136 B7 B7
Duckles 67–852; Duckles 74–1184

A dictionary catalog, including composers with their works listed, and also title entries (but works in anthologies are cited only under main entry, not individually by title). Strongest in nineteenth century. About 5,500 volumes altogether. See 0228.

Boston. Public Library. **Dictionary Catalog of the Music Collection.** See 0228.

0374   British Broadcasting Corporation. Central Music Library. **Chamber Music Catalogue; Chamber Music, Violin and Keyboard, Cello and Keyboard, Various.** London: British Broadcasting Corp., 1965. 1v. (various pagings). ML128 C4 B7
Duckles 67–610; Duckles 74–801

Includes some 24,000 items, under composers. Information on arrangers (if any), publishers, and durations.

0375   British Broadcasting Corporation. Central Music Library. **Piano and Organ Catalogue.** 1965. 2v. ML128 P3 B7
Duckles 74–801

Seven parts, each in composer order: piano solo, piano duet, piano trio, two or more pianos, left or right hand only, organ solo, organ with other instrument(s). Total of 48,000 entries, with same facts given as for 0374.

0376   British Broadcasting Corporation. Central Music Library. **Song Catalogue.** 1966. 4v. ML128 S3 B7
Duckles 74–801

Two volumes by composer, two by title. Mostly solo songs with keyboard accompaniment; also songs with no accompaniment, duets with and without accompaniment, recitations with piano, songs with other instruments, some popular/folk/national/patriotic songs. About 140,000 entries. Same data as in 0374.

0377   British Broadcasting Corporation. **Choral and Opera Catalogue.** 1967. 2v. ML128 V7 B76
Duckles 74–801

Composer and title lists; lists of works in more than eight parts; works with instrumental obbligati; non-operatic works with children's voices; libretti. Some 60,000 titles. Comparable information to that in 0374.

The preceding four items give access to much of the content of the world's largest performance library. Both published and unpublished material is listed. These catalogs are ideal starting points in identification searches and in compiling groups of pieces with some common characteristic.

0378   British Museum. Department of Printed Books. Hirsch Library. **Music in the Hirsch Library**. London: Trustees of the British Museum, 1951. 438p. (Catalogue of Printed Books in the British Museum, Accessions, Part 53). ML136 L8 B73 pt53
Duckles 67–973; Duckles 74–1334
The original catalog of this major collection (0231) was rich in bibliographic detail, but did not include more than a third of the holdings. All 9,000 musical items are in the present catalog: vocal scores, operas, orchestral scores, collections. A supplement appeared in 1959 (0230).

0379   Brussels. Conservatoire Royal de Musique. Bibliothèque. **Catalogue de la Bibliothèque** ... Par A. Wotquenne. Bruxelles: Coosemans, 1898-1912. 4v. Annexe I. *Libretti d'opéras et oratorios italiens du XVIIe siècle*. Bruxelles: O. Schepens, 1901. 189p. ML136 B9 C78
Duckles 67–859; Duckles 74–1194
A very large general collection, covering manuscripts and printed music; classified arrangement.

0380   Durham Cathedral. Library. **A Catalogue of the Printed Music and Books on Music in Durham Cathedral Library**. By R. Alec Harman. London: Oxford University Press, 1968. xv, 136p. ML136 D909
Duckles 74–1229; Winchell 67–2BH4
A small but valuable collection with many rarities. About a sixth of the 682 items listed are unique in Great Britain. Vocal, instrumental and theoretical works in separate lists; indexes to persons, titles, and first lines.

Hirsch, Paul. **Katalog der Musikbibliothek** ...
See 0231.

0381   Iowa. University. Library. **An Annotated Catalog of Rare Musical Items in the Libraries of the University of Iowa**. By Frederick K. Gable ... Iowa City: University of Iowa Libraries, 1963. viii, 130p. Supplement, 1973.
Duckles 67–922; Duckles 74–1275
Base volume describes 275 items, both scores and books. Name and subject indexes. Supplement adds 278 new entries.

0382   Liverpool Central Libraries. **Catalogue of the Music Library**. Liverpool: the Libraries, 1954. iv, 572p. ML136 L7 M83
Duckles 67–963; Duckles 74–1322
Thorough dictionary catalog of a very sizeable (45,000 entries) general collection, scores and books, mostly post-Bach. Contents notes; instrumentation for orchestral scores.

0383 Madrid. Biblioteca Nacional. **Catálogo musical de la Biblioteca Nacional de Madrid.** Por Higinio Anglés y José Subirá. Barcelona: Consejo Superior de Investigaciones Científicas, Instituto Español de Musicología, 1946-51. 3v. (Catálogos de la Musica Antigua Conservada en España, 1-3). ML136 M16 B5
Duckles 67—996; Duckles 74—1360
A list of 856 items, with considerable bibliographic detail. Subject arranged, with name and subject indexes.

New York (City). Public Library. Reference Department. **Dictionary Catalog of the Music Collection . . .**
See 0233.

National Union Catalog: Pre-1956 Imprints.
See 0240.

0384 Paris. Bibliothèque Sainte-Geneviève. **Catalogue du fonds musical . . .** Ed. Madeleine Garros and Simone Wallon. Kassel: Internationale Vereinigung der Musikbibliotheken; Internationale Gesellschaft für Musikwissenschaft, 1967. xi, 156p. (Catalogus Musicus, 4). ML113 C35
Duckles 74—1429
Descriptive list of 502 printed works and 79 manuscripts. Particularly rich in French and Italian composers.

0385 Pazdirek, Franz. **Universal-Handbuch der Musikliteratur aller Zeiten und Völker . . .** Wien: Pazdirek & Co., 1904-1910. 14v. (Reprint—Hilversum: Frits Knuf, 1967. 12v.). ML113 U6
Duckles 67—641; Duckles 74—818
One of the monumental lists, containing some 500,000 titles. Composer sequence, with source, price, and publisher of each piece. International in scope; primarily Europe and United States. Concentrates on music in print at the time, thus giving an emphasis to late nineteenth century publications.

0386 Philadelphia. Free Library. **The Edwin A. Fleisher Music Collection** . . . Philadelphia: Privately printed, 1965— . (1st ed. 1933-45. 2v. Supplementary list, 1945-55. Philadelphia, 1955? 33p. ML136 P4 F7
Duckles 67—1053; Duckles 74—1437
Catalog of a lending library which contains scores and parts for some 4,000 orchestral works and 2,500 works for solo instruments with orchestra. Arranged in 15 classes. For each title: publisher, instrumentation, duration, composition date, and first performance. Composer and arranger index.

0387 U.S. Library of Congress. **Library of Congress Catalog—Music, Books on Music, and Sound Recordings** (formerly *Music and Phonorecords*), 1953— . Washington: the Library, 1953— . (semiannual; annual and quinquennial cumulations). Z881 U52 M8
Duckles 67—653; Duckles 74—835

Scores and sound recordings of all types, current and retrospective, cataloged by L.C. or cooperating libraries. Composer order, with name and subject indexes. The principal international listing of music now being issued periodically.

0388   U.S. Library of Congress. Music Division. **Dramatic Music: Catalogue of Full Scores**. Compiled by Oscar G. T. Sonneck. Washington, the Library, 1908. 170p. (Reprint—New York: Da Capo Press, 1969). (Da Capo Press Music Reprint Series). ML136 L3 D7
        Duckles 67—1121; Duckles 74—1536; ARBA 70—II, 27
Some 1,300 scores of operas, ballets, and incidental music for plays, in composer order. Includes manuscripts, printed editions, and some photocopies. Title-page information given, descriptive comments on manuscripts, first performance data.

0389   U.S. Library of Congress. Music Division. **Orchestral Music Catalogue: Scores** ... Prepared under the direction of Oscar G. T. Sonneck. Washington: Government Printing Office, 1912. 663p. (Reprint—New York: Da Capo Press, 1969). (Da Capo Press Music Reprint Series). ML136 L3 O6
        Duckles 67—1122; Duckles 74—1538; ARBA 70—II, 27
Composer list of full scores, with subject and title indexes. Mostly nineteenth century works. About 4,000 items; imprint data, some citations to relevant literature and explanatory comments. Instrumentation not given.

Warsaw. Uniwersytet. Biblioteka. **Katalog** ...
See 0237.

Wolffheim, Werner J., Library. **Versteigerung** ...
See 0238.

GUIDES TO COLLECTED EDITIONS

Under this umbrella we have clustered all those grand anthologies, sets of complete works by individual composers, and national or historical compilations of music. The present section deals only with guides and bibliographies of the genre; attention to the editions themselves is reserved for Volumes 4, 5, and 6.
        The basic guide is:

0390   Heyer, Anna Harriet. **Historical Sets, Collected Editions, and Monuments of Music: A Guide to Their Contents**. 2d ed. Chicago: American Library Association, 1969. (1st ed. 1957). xiv, 573p. ML113 H52 1969
        Duckles 67—730 (for 1st ed.); Duckles 74—1028; Winchell 67—3BH5
A descriptive listing, in title order, of some 900 sets. Indication is given of contents in each volume (e.g., "Vol. 1. Mayr, Rupert Ignaz.

Ausgewählte Kirchenmusik") but individual titles of pieces are not located. Composer index sometimes identifies particular pieces, but most often points to groups (e.g., "Naich, Robert. Lieder. In: Publikationen älterer praktischer und theoretischer Musikwerke Jahrg. 1-3"). Index also signals certain forms —e.g., Dances, Chansonniers, Chant.

The next item is a convenient companion to Heyer:

0391   Charles, Sydney Robinson. **A Handbook of Music and Music Literature in Sets and Series**. New York: Free Press, 1972. 497p. ML113 C45
        Duckles 74–1020; ARBA 73–1029
This compilation is more selective (197 music editions) and more descriptive than 0390. In addition to music collections, gives titles in 82 monograph series, some of them not in Blum (0357). Also describes publishing history of 61 journals (see note after 0330).

Other lists and guides now follow in author order:

Apel, Willi. **Editions, Historical**. In *Harvard Dictionary* . . . (0002), pp. 253-82.
Gives contents and bibliographic data on 53 collected editions considered most valuable for musicological research.

Azhderian, Helen Wentworth. **Reference Works** . . . (0226).
Includes list of 360 editions.

0392   Broude Brothers Limited. **Collected Editions, Historical Sets, Reference Works, Thematic Catalogues, Periodicals, Reprints; Catalogue 105**. New York: Broude Brothers Limited, 1973. iii, 57p.
A convenient gathering of major sets, available without cost from the publisher. Contents of each volume given, in the manner of 0390. Supersedes several earlier catalogs of this material by Broude.

0393   Coover, James B. **Gesamtausgaben: A Checklist** . . . n.p., Distant Press, 1970. iii, 27 l. ML113 C66
        Duckles 74–1021
Lists all editions with claim to completeness, except single-medium compilations (e.g., Gibbons' keyboard works). Much duplication with 0390, but does have some items not found there, such as the works of Manuel Cardoso and Hanns Eisler. Total of 376 entries.

0394   De Lerma, Dominique-René. **A Checklist of Collected Works in Print and in Progress**. 3rd ed. Bloomington, Ind.: the Author. (typescript).
Cited in 0210.

0395   Loyan, Richard. **An Index to Selected Anthologies of Music**. Goleto, Calif.: the Author, preface dated 1964. iii, 55 l. ML113 L69
Indexes anthologies compiled by Bartha, Della Corte, Einstein, Schering, Apel, etc.

0396   Schmieder, Wolfgang. **Denkmäler der Tonkunst.** In MGG (0058), 3,
        cols. 164-92. **Gesamtausgaben.** 4, cols. 1850-76. ML100 M92
        Duckles 67–724, 729; Duckles 74–1022
        Describes 213 major editions and gives contents in the *Denkmäler*
article, 84 in the other.

LISTS OF MANUSCRIPT MUSIC

Many of the sources presented in this section could well have been
held for the section that follows (on pre-1800 music), since a large number of
musical manuscripts are indeed from early periods. However, it was thought
useful to gather manuscript bibliographies in one place first, and then to cite
them a second time where appropriate in later sections. Specialized lists (e.g.,
the Breslauer catalog *Das Deutsche Lied*) and strictly national lists (e.g.,
Linker's *Music of the Minnesinger ...*) are reserved for later volumes;
likewise lists pertaining to individual composers.

0397   Albrecht, Otto. **A Census of Autograph Music Manuscripts of
        European Composers in American Libraries.** Philadelphia: University
        of Pennsylvania Press, 1953. 331p. ML135 A2 A4
        Duckles 67–736; Duckles 74–1530
        Descriptive inventory of 2,017 manuscripts by 517 composers.
Identifies owners and former owners, gives bibliographic details. One special
use is the possibility of discovering the date on which a given piece was
completed; also dedications and other remarks by the composers.

        Apel, Willi. **Sources, Musical (pre-1450).** In *Harvard Dictionary ...*
        (0002), pp. 797-99. ML100 A64 1969.
        Duckles 74–1036
        Describes 27 major depositories of manuscript music, with refer-
ences to writings about them. Locations, modern editions cited.

0398   Arnese, Raffaele. **I codici notati della Biblioteca Nazionale di
        Napoli.** Firenze: Leo Olschki, 1967. 257p. (Biblioteca di Bibliografia
        Italiana ... 47). ML93 A76
        Duckles 74–1394
        A remarkably detailed accounting of 85 items, spanning the tenth to
eighteenth centuries. Illustrates various notational styles in liturgical manuscripts; 33 plates. Omits Byzantine material, which was surveyed in an article
by L. Tardo in *Accademie e Biblioteche d'Italia* 1 (February 1938)– .

0399   Besseler, Heinrich. "Studien zur Musik des Mittelalters: 1. Neue
        Quellen des 14. und Beginnenden 15. Jahrhunderts. 2. Die Motette
        von Franko von Köln bis Philipp von Vitry." *Archiv für Musik-
        wissenschaft,* 7 (1925), 167-252; 9 (1927), 137-258. ML5 A63
        Duckles 67–740; Duckles 74–1038
        Lists and descriptions of the key late medieval sources.

0400   Bohn, Emil. **Die musikalischen Handschriften des XVI. und XVII. Jahrhunderts in der Stadtbibliothek zu Breslau** ... Breslau: Julius Hainauer, 1890. xvi, 423p. (Reprint—Hildesheim: Georg Olms, 1970). ML136 B8 B6
        Duckles 67—1127; Duckles 74—1546
Descriptive list of 356 items. Excellent indexes: individual titles, anonyma, titles under composer names; vocal incipits. No facsimiles. See also 0422.

0401   British Museum. Department of Manuscripts. **Catalogue of Manuscript Music in the British Museum, by Augustus Hughes-Hughes.** London: the Trustees, 1906-1909. 3v. (Reprint—1964). ML136 L8 B722
        Duckles 67—968; Duckles 74—1328
Contents: v. 1, Sacred music; v. 2, Secular vocal music; v. 3, Instrumental music, treatises, etc. Each volume classified, with author, subject, and title indexes. Also first-line index for songs, and an index by manuscript number. A vast collection with great variety of material; for instance, some of the genres in v. 1 are anthems, burial services, canons, cantatas, glees, and graces before meals. Continued by the next item.

0402   British Museum. **Handlist of Music Manuscripts Acquired 1908-67.** Prepared by Pamela J. Willetts. London: British Museum, 1970. vii, 112p. ML135 L65 B7
        Duckles 74—1329
Continues 0401. Arranged by year of acquisition, with composer
index.

0403   Corbin, Solange. **Répertoire de manuscrits médiévaux contenant des notations musicales.** Paris: Éditions du Centre National de la Recherche Scientifique, 1965— . v. 1— . 157p. ML135 A2 C67
        Duckles 74—1052
Volume 1 gives holdings of the Bibliothèque Sainte-Geneviève, Paris, edited by Madeleine Bernard. Very detailed descriptions, with 26 plates. Volume 2 covers the Bibliothèque Mazarine.

0404   Florence. Biblioteca Nazionale Centrale. **Catalogo dei manoscritti musicali** ... Ed. Bianca Becherini. Kassel, New York: Bärenreiter, 1959. xii, 177p. ML136 F56 B5
        Duckles 67—890; Duckles 74—1233
An important collection of major composers, though only 144 items are presented. Excellent descriptions and indexes. Title of all works given within collections; citations to literature; first line index of poems; personal name index.

0405   Frere, W. H. **A Descriptive Handlist of the Musical and Latin-Liturgical Mss. of the Middle Ages Preserved in the Libraries of Great Britain and Ireland ... Printed for the Members of the Plainsong and**

Mediaeval Music Society . . . London: B. Quaritch, 1901-1932. 2v. (Reprint–Hildesheim: Georg Olms, 1967). ML135 B5
Duckles 67–741; Duckles 74–1039
Detailed descriptions of 1,031 manuscripts. Arranged by library, with personal and geographical indexes; 17 plates.

0406   Geering, Arnold. **Die Organa und mehrstimmigen Conductus in den Handschriften des deutschen Sprachgebietes vom 13. bis 16. Jahrhundert.** Bern: P. Haupt, 1952. xv, 99p. (Publikationen der Schweizerischen Musikforschenden Gesellschaft, ser. 2, 1). ML174 G37
Duckles 67–765; Duckles 74–1070
Contents of 73 sources of early polyphony in Holland and German-speaking countries. Arranged by library, sublisted by manuscript number. Individual titles within large manuscripts are given, and the type of notation is mentioned. Works are discussed by genre in a separate section. Some musical transcriptions.

0407   Gennrich, Friedrich. **Bibliographie der ältesten französischen und lateinischen Motetten.** Darmstadt: Selbstverlag [Gennrich], 1957. lii, 124p. (Summa Musicae Medii Aevi, 2). ML128 S2 G4
Duckles 67–766; Duckles 74–1071
Contents and library locations for 1,219 numbered items, which are the basic repertoire of the thirteenth century motet. Arranged by tenor; index of tenor sources and tenor texts; incipits; references to modern editions and literature. Continues the inventory work of Ludwig, 0412.

0408   Kümmerling, H. **Katalog der Sammlung Bokemeyer.** Kassel: Bärenreiter, 1970. 423p. (Kieler Schriften zur Musikwissenschaft, 18). ML97 B64 K8
Duckles 74–1170
Some composers with strong representation in this excellent manuscript collection are Bononcini, Gasparini, and the Scarlattis. Number of items: 1,839; incipits, first-line index, 105 facsimiles. Also an unusual section illustrating watermarks.

0409   Lisbon. Palacio da Ajuda. Biblioteca. **Catálogo de música manuscrita . . . Elaborado sob a Direccão de Mariana Amélia Machado Santos** . . . Lisboa: Palacio da Ajuda, 1958-63. 6v. ML136 L68 P3
Duckles 67–961; Duckles 74–1320
Composer list of 3,617 manuscript items, mostly eighteenth and nineteenth century, strong in Italian opera. Many Portuguese composers.

0410   Llorens, Josephus. **Capellae Sixtinae codices musicis notis instructi sive praelo excussi** . . . Roma, Città del Vaticano: Biblioteca Apostolica Vaticana, 1960. xxii, 555p. (Studi e Testi, 202). ML136 R72 S57
Duckles 67–1071; Duckles 74–1505

Page-by-page description of some 600 items; texts, incipits, name and term indexes. Strongest in material from the sixteenth to the eighteenth centuries. Ten facsimile plates.

0411 Ludwig, Friedrich. "Die Quellen der Motetten ältesten Stils." *Archiv für Musikwissenschaft*, 5 (1923), 185-222, 273-315. ML5 A63
Duckles 67–779; Duckles 74–1086
Contents of about 50 thirteenth century manuscripts. See note at 0412.

0412 Ludwig, Friedrich. **Repertorium organorum recentioris et motetorum vetustissimi stili.** Band 1: Catalogue Raisonné der Quellen. Abteilung 1: Handschriften in Quadrat-Notation. Halle: Niemeyer, 1910. 344p. Abteilung 2: Handschriften in Mensuralnotation. Besorgt von Friedrich Gennrich. Langen bei Frankfurt, 1961. (Summa Musicae Medii Aevi, 7). 0411 reprinted as a supplement. Band 1: "2. erweiterte Auflage," ed. Luther A. Dittmer. New York: Institute of Mediaeval Music; Hildesheim: Georg Olms, 1964. xix, 348p. (Abteilung 1 only). ML128 M3 L9

Band 2: Musikalisches Anfangs-Verzeichnis des nach Tenores geordneten Repertorium. Besorgt von Friedrich Gennrich. Langen bei Frankfurt: 1961-62. 71p. (Summa Musicae Medii Aevi, 8).
Duckles 67–780; Duckles 74–1087
This group of inventories covers many of the essential sources of thirteenth century organa and motets. The four principal manuscripts for study of the "Notre Dame school" are given close attention: Wolfenbüttel 677 and 1099, Laurenziana pluteus 29, and Madrid Bibl. Nac. 20486 (formerly, as cited by Ludwig, Hh 167). Very detailed, page-by-page accounts of everything in the manuscripts, with concordances and references to scholarly literature. No musical illustrations; no indexes. Band 2, drawn by Gennrich from unfinished copy of Ludwig, gives the thematic material of 515 motets.

0413 Munich. Bayerische Staatsbibliothek. **Die musikalischen Handschriften der K. Hof- und Staatsbibliothek** . . . Beschrieben von Jul. Jos. Maier. Erster Theil: Die Handschriften bis zum Ende des XVII. Jahrhunderts. München: in Commission der Palm'schen Hofbuchhandlung, 1879. 176p. Z6621 M91 vol. 8
Duckles 67–1017; Duckles 74–1390
Some 6,380 compositions are listed, in 278 anthologies and choirbooks. An important source for the sixteenth century.

0414 Oxford. Bodleian Library. **Medieval Polyphony in the Bodleian Library, by Dom Anselm Hughes.** Oxford: Bodleian Library, 1951. 63p. ML136 O9 H9
Duckles 67–1031; Duckles 74–1412
Descriptions of 51 manuscripts (including the Canonici Misc. 213).

Incipits, references to modern editions and literature. First-line index of texts; index to composers and places of origin.

> Paris. Bibliothèque Nationale. Département des Imprimés. **Catalogue du fonds de musique ancienne** . . .
> See 0253. Compositions are in composer order, with no indexes. Incipits or brief thematics (one measure or so for vocal pieces; three or four measures for instrumental pieces). Most of Volumes 1 and 2 devoted to anonymous "airs."

0415   Pierpont Morgan Library, New York. **The Mary Flagler Cary Music Collection.** New York: Pierpont Morgan Library, 1970. xii, 158, 108p. ML136 N52 P5
      Duckles 74—1407; ARBA 72—1104
      Excellent small collection of manuscript music (163 pieces, from Bach to Schoenberg) and 3,000 letters and documents (Bach, Beethoven, Brahms, Caruso, Jenny Lind, etc., etc.). Annotations by Otto Albrecht; 49 plates.

0416   Tenbury Wells, England. St. Michael's College. Library. **The Catalogue of Manuscripts in the Library** . . . Compiled by E. H. Fellowes. Paris: Éditions de l'Oiseau Lyre, 1934. 319p. ML136 T4 S3
      Duckles 67—1085; Duckles 74—1483
      A varied collection of 1,386 numbered pieces (the Ouseley bequest) plus a group of manuscripts and printed books dealing with eighteenth century French opera (the Toulouse-Philidor Collection). Detailed descriptions with all individual compositions named. Most of the material is seventeenth to nineteenth centuries; however, there are some interesting earlier items, such as an index to the masses of Lassus, written by the composer. The composers represented are mostly English and Italian; there is a name index.

0417   Vienna. Nationalbibliothek. **Tabulae codicum manuscriptorum praeter graecos et orientales in Bibliotheca Palatina Vindobonensi asservatorum** . . . Compiled by Joseph Mantuani. Vindobonae [Wien]: C. Geroldi Filius, 1897-99. 2v. in 1; x, 587p. ML136 V6 H8
      Duckles 67—1114; Duckles 74—1526
      Inventory of 4,000 musical manuscripts in the Library, in call-number sequence; name and title indexes, text incipits. Text in Latin.

0418   Vienna. Nationalbibliothek. Musiksammlung. Archiv für Photogramme musikalischer Meisterhandschriften. **Katalog des Archivs für Photogramme musikalischer Meisterhandschriften.** Bearb. von Agnes Ziffer. Wien: Georg Prachner Verlag, 1967. xxiv, 483p. ML136 V6 N45
      Duckles 74—1527
      Manuscripts of the major Viennese masters, in composer order. Descriptive commentaries and citations to literature. Sketches and notebooks are included with completed works.

LISTS OF EARLY MUSIC (TO 1800)

The designation "early music" has come to be applied to works written before the nineteenth century. Bibliographically as well as stylistically, the period around 1800 marked a boundary line through music history; up to that time the output of composers was somehow comprehensible in its aggregate vastness. Libraries found it feasible to inventory their holdings of that early music: e.g., British Museum (0248) and others in Britain (0426), and Bibliothèque National (0253). Individual scholars like Eitner (0187) and Lott (0435) have confronted the era. As the nineteenth century advanced, it became less practical to keep track of all that was being composed. Actually many of the lists in this section are confined to a still earlier cutoff date, 1700.

In a sense, the few titles cited in this section, and in the preceding section on manuscripts, form the collective cornerstone of historical musicology. Early music is the raw material of that noble discipline; tools for unearthing old scores, for identifying and organizing them, are bibliographical. Interpretation, evaluation, and understanding—which are the higher purposes of musicology—cannot occur without the preliminary mining efforts of patient scholars in the bibliographic terrain.

Surely the most important bibliographic exploration in early music is this one, still in progress:

0419 **Répertoire internationale des sources musicales. Internationales Quellenlexikon der Musik. International Inventory of Musical Sources.** München: G. Henle; London: Novello; Kassel: Bärenreiter, 1960– . ML113 I6

Duckles 67–774, 775, 776; Duckles 74–779, 780, 1079 to 1084

This massive project of the International Musicological Society and the International Association of Music Libraries began in 1952 under the chairmanship of Friedrich Blume. The purpose of RISM—the usual acronym—is to present a complete bibliography of musical works, published or not, which appeared in all countries up to the year 1800. Writings about music are also being listed. RISM is being issued in two series: A (composer order) and B (by type or format). More than 1,000 libraries in 30 countries are represented in the survey, and each item listed is located via symbols in one or more of those libraries. Completion of publication is planned for the mid-70s. These volumes have appeared:

Series A. V. 1-3, **Einzeldrucke vor 1800**. (Aarts-Gyrowetz, to date).

Series B. V. 1/1. Lesure, François. **Recueils imprimés: XVIe-XVIIe siècles, 1—Liste Chronologique**. 1960.

V. 2. Lesure, François. **Recueils imprimés: XVIIIe siècle**. 1964. Supplement in *Notes*, 28/3 (March 1972), 397-418.

V.3/1. Smits van Waesberghe. **The Theory of Music from the Carolingian Era up to 1400**. Part 1. 1961. See 0255.

V.4/1. Reaney, Gilbert. **Manuscripts of Polyphonic Music (ca. 1320-1400)**. 1969.

V.4/3-4. Fischer, Kurt von. **Handschriften mit mehrstimmiger Musik des 14. 15. und 16. Jahrhunderts.** 1972.

V.5/1. Husmann, Heinrich. **Tropen- und Sequenzhandschriften.** 1964.

V.6/1-2. Lesure, François. **Écrits imprimés concernant la musique.** 1971.

Series A will cover some 8,000 composers, listing all known works with library locations and biliographic data. It is planned for six to eight volumes. A second section of Series A will also be issued: a catalog of pre-1800 manuscripts. This series is thus intended to be a replacement for Eitner's *Quellen-Lexikon* (0187). Some 200,000 items will be covered.

Series B aims to replace another Eitner list, the *Bibliographie der Musik-Sammelwerke* (0420). V. 1/1 is a chronological list of some 2,700 music collections (publications including the works of more than one composer) issued between 1501 and 1700, with contents and locations, indexed by printers, editors, authors, and titles. V. 1/2 will present incipits of the pieces in those same collections.

V. 2 of Series B extends the range that Eitner had spanned, by listing some 1,800 collections printed between 1701 and 1801—also with imprint data, locations, and contents. This volume is in title sequence. V. 3/1 (0255) is first of a series that will cover various countries; it contains lists of Latin treatises from Austria, Belgium, Switzerland, Denmark, France, Luxembourg, and the Netherlands. Arrangement is by present library location.

V. 4 lists manuscripts from the eleventh through the fourteenth centuries, aiming to cover all known polyphonic material. About 400 items, from Europe and the United States, are meticulously described, with incipits, citations to literature, and commentaries. Composer and text-first-line indexes. Arranged by library.

In Parts 3 and 4 the time range is extended through the sixteenth century for organal polyphony.

V. 5/1 lists and describes trope and sequence manuscripts, grouping them by country of present location. Information given on bibliographical details, provenance, notation; citations to literature. Name, place, and subject indexes.

V. 6/1-2 is an author list of brief title entries, with publishers and locations. Valuable indexes by date and printer/publisher. Marred by numerous inconsistencies and errors; cf. review in *Notes*, 30 (Sept. 1973), 54-57. Even when RISM Series A is completed, its predecessor will still be of use for information not provided in the newer work:

Eitner, Robert. **Biographisch-bibliographisches Quellen-Lexikon** . . . See 0187.

The other Eitner work paralleled by RISM (Series B., v. 1/1) is:

0420   Eitner, Robert. **Bibliographie der Musik-Sammelwerke des XVI. und XVII. Jahrhunderts**. Berlin: L. Liepmannssohn, 1877. 964p. (Reprint—Hildesheim: Georg Olms, 1963). ML114 E36

Duckles 67—759; Duckles 74—1064

A chronological list of collections issued from 1501 to 1700, about 1,200 of them. Bibliographic descriptions, contents, library locations. First-line index of vocal texts, composer and printer indexes. Indexes and details not given in RISM.

Other important bibliographies for the early period are now presented in alphabetical sequence.

0421   Becker, Carl Ferdinand. **Die Tonwerke des XVI. und XVII. Jahrhunderts; oder, systematisch-chronologische Zusammenstellung der in diesen zwei Jahrhunderten gedruckten Musikalien.** 2 . . . Ausgabe. Leipzig: E. Fleischer, 1855. (1st ed. 1847). xiii, 358 cols. (Reprint—Hildesheim: Georg Olms, 1969). ML114 B39

Duckles 67—739; Duckles 74—1037

More than 4,000 entries, most of them multiple: either collections representing several composers, or publications with a number of pieces by one composer—but some entries are single pieces. Arrangement is by type or by instrument, and within each category by date; this plan is a useful adjunct, for modern investigators, to what is found in RISM and 0420. Information generally limited to imprint data and contents.

0422   Bohn, Emil. **Bibliographie der Musik-Druckwerke bis 1700, welche in der Stadtbibliothek, der Bibliothek des Academischen Instituts für Kirchenmusik und der Königlichen und Universitäts Bibliothek zu Breslau aufbewahrt werden** . . . Berlin: A. Cohn, 1883. viii, 450p. (Reprint—Hildesheim: Georg Olms, 1969). ML136 B8 B5

Duckles 67—1126; Duckles 74—1545

About 1,500 musical works printed before 1700, in composer order within large categories. Good bibliographic descriptions; but titles of individual pieces within collections are not given (some indication of contents generally presented). Strongest in German and Italian vocal and liturgical compositions. Also lists some 60 theoretical treatises. Not illustrated. See also 0400.

0423   Breitkopf und Härtel. **The Breitkopf Thematic Catalogue: The Six Parts and Sixteen Supplements, 1762-1787.** Edited and with an introduction and indexes by Barry S. Brook. New York: Dover Publications, 1966. xxvii p., 888 cols., xxxi-lxxxi p. ML145 B8315

Duckles 67—952; Duckles 74—1043

This was the earliest thematic catalog, originally issued in 22 parts over a 25-year period. Around 15,000 incipits are included, by about 1,000 composers, with information about each piece (instrumentation, text, dates, etc.). In the Brook edition, emendations and commentaries are added. Further corrigenda are reported to be in progress by Professor Brook.

British Museum. Department of Printed Books. **Catalogue of Printed Music Published between 1487 and 1800** . . .

See 0248. An international list, strongest in British material. Arranged in composer-title sequence. Includes music published in periodicals (see also 0424).

0424   British Museum. Department of Printed Books. **Hand-List of Music Published in Some British and Foreign Periodicals between 1787 and 1848, Now in the British Museum.** London: Trustees of the British Museum, 1962. 80p.

       Duckles 67–971; Duckles 74–1046

Adds to the coverage of periodicals in 0248, extending the time period and adding 12 journals (seven of them German). A composer and anonymous-title arrangement of 1,855 entries; mostly songs.

0425   British Museum. King's Music Library. **Catalogue of the King's Music Library, by William Barclay Squire and Hilda Andrews.** London: Printed by order of the Trustees, 1927-29. 3v. ML138 B8 K4

       Duckles 67–975; Duckles 74–1336

Part I: *The Handel Manuscripts.* xi, 143p. (Discussed in Volume 4 of the present work.) Part II: *The Miscellaneous Manuscripts.* x, 277p. Mostly eighteenth century material; rich in Italian opera. Composer sequence, without title index. Part III: *Printed Music and Musical Literature.* 383p. Music and books in one author-composer alphabet; no indexes.

0426   **British Union-Catalogue of Early Music Printed before the Year 1801: A Record of the Holdings of Over One Hundred Libraries throughout the British Isles.** Ed. Edith B. Schnapper. London: Butterworths Scientific Publications, 1957. 2v. ML116 B7

       Duckles 67–747; Duckles 74–1047

About 55,000 items: separately published compositions, music printed in books or periodicals; psalters and hymnals which contain music. Incorporates titles from 0248 and adds later acquisitions of the British Museum, which accounts for 60 percent of all the entries. Arrangement by composer, with anonymous titles and certain genre groupings interfiled. Popular sheet music included, but not exhaustively—for other categories comprehensiveness was the goal. Information given: bibliographic description, library location. An outstanding feature is the thorough title index, which makes possible identification of songs and other pieces. It should be noticed that while the libraries inventoried are British, the contents of this catalog are from many countries, in various languages.

0427   Brown, Howard Mayer. **Instrumental Music Printed before 1600: A Bibliography.** Cambridge: Harvard University Press, 1965. 559p. ML128 I65 B77

       Duckles 67–749; Duckles 74–1049

A chronological list of some 400 collections, including purely instrumental music and music for instruments with voice. Bibliographical descriptions and commentaries; references to secondary literature and modern editions. Cites lost works as well as those extant. Indexes by library, type of notation, medium, personal names, first lines, and titles.

0428   Brussels. Bibliothèque Royale de Belgique. **Catalogue de la Bibliothèque de F. J. Fétis** . . . Bruxelles: C. Muquardt, 1877. xi, 946p. ML136 B9 B5

      Duckles 67–856; Duckles 74–1190

The working library of a great scholar (cf. 0190); 7,325 items of music and writings on music, as well as general titles. See also 0429.

0429   Brussels. Bibliothèque Royale de Belgique. **Catalogue des imprimés musicaux des XVe, XVIe et XVIIe siècles. Fonds général. Par Bernard Huys.** Bruxelles: Bibliothèque Royale de Belgique, 1965. xiv, 422p. ML136 B9 B543

      Duckles 67–857; Duckles 74–1191

A detailed descriptive list of 446 numbered items, generally excluding material in 0428. Composer or anthology-title order, with composer index. Special value attaches to the title index, which covers all works in anthologies and even in theoretical treatises. Some facsimiles and commentaries.

0430   Davidsson, Åke. **Catalogue critique et descriptif des imprimés de musique des XVIe et XVIIe siècles conservés dans les bibliothèques suédoises (excepté la Bibliothèque de l'Université Royale d'Upsala).** Upsala: Almquist & Wiksells, 1952. 471p. (Studia Musicologica Upsaliensia, 1). ML136 A1 D3

      Duckles 67–753; Duckles 74–1057

Descriptive list of 534 numbered items located in 18 Swedish libraries; supplementing an earlier inventory of the University of Upsala collection (0438). Arrangement by composer and anthology-title. Full imprint data, contents of each publication (but no title index to individual works in collections or anthologies). Index to printers and to place of publication. Citations to literature.

0431   Eitner, Robert. **Verzeichnis neuer Ausgaben alter Musikwerke aus der frühesten Zeit bis zum Jahre 1800.** Berlin: Trautwein, 1871. 208p. (*Monatshefte für Musikgeschichte.* Beilage. 1871). Nachträge in *Monatshefte* 9 (1877), Beilage 1877, 10 (1878).

      Duckles 67–728; Duckles 74–1026

A survey of collected editions and of historical-theoretical works published up to Eitner's day, attempting to identify those with pre-1800 music in them. Main list is in editor-title sequence; information given for each entry is imprint data and names of composers whose works are included—not specific titles of their compositions. Another list does locate individual titles, under names of composers, in whichever collections they appear. There are special indexes of German secular song and sacred song. Spot-comparison with Heyer (0390) indicates many collections cited by Eitner which do not appear there; however, for items covered in both bibliographies, Heyer gives more complete accountings of pieces within.

0432 **Fontes artis musicae**. Paris: International Association of Music Libraries, 1954– . (three per year).
Duckles 67–726; Duckles 74–582
Regular feature is list of "Éditions et Rééditions de Musique Ancienne (avant 1800)," which offers brief information about European and American publications. Generally restricted to imprint data; does not identify composers in anthologies, nor titles found in works devoted to a single composer.

0433 Henry E. Huntington Library and Art Gallery, San Marino, California. **Catalogue of Music in the Huntington Library Printed before 1801**. Compiled by Edythe N. Backus. San Marino: the Library, 1949. ix, 773p. ML138 H35
Duckles 67–1076; Duckles 74–1468
A composer and anonymous-title list of musical works in various kinds of publications, including periodicals. Emphasizes British music, but includes some incunabula and Americana. Total of 2,368 main entries. Chronological index, and–possibly the most valuable feature–a 393-page index to first lines of all songs and operatic arias.

0434 Krummel, Donald W. **Printed Music, 1501-1700: A Bibliographical Conspectus**. Urbana, Ill.: the Author. (typescript)
Cited in 0210; but reference to publication by University Microfilms should be disregarded. Arranges all printed musical editions by country, city, publisher, and date. To be published as part of a larger study of early music printing.

0435 Lott, Walter. **Verzeichnis der Neudrucke alter Musik** ... Leipzig: Hofmeister, 1937-43. 7v.
Duckles 67–735; Duckles 74–1034
Annual lists, for the years 1936-42, of publications of pre-1800 music. Large and small works, separates and parts of collections, transcriptions and arrangements. Arrangement by composer within each year; classified and title indexes. Strongest for German editions.

Paris. Conservatoire National ... **Catalogue** ...
See 0254.

0436 Paris. Conservatoire National de Musique et de Déclamation. Fonds Blancheton. ... **Inventaire critique du Fonds Blancheton** ... Paris: E. Droz, 1930-31. 2v. (Publications de la Société Française de Musicologie, 2. sér., 2: 1-2). ML136 P2 C74
Duckles 67–1048; Duckles 74–1431
This collection includes about 300 instrumental works, by 104 composers, issued before 1750. Important early symphonists, as well as minor

figures, are found (Abaco, Biarello, Brioschi, Monn, etc.). Brief thematics are presented for each movement of each work, and some extended musical examples are provided. There are also bibliographic descriptions, biographical sketches, and an index by genre.

0437   Sartori, Claudio. **Bibliografia della musica strumentale italiana stampata in Italia fino al 1700.** Con pref. di Alfred Einstein. Firenze: L. S. Olschki, 1952-68. 2v. (Biblioteca di Bibliografia Italiana, 23, 56). ML190 I8 S3
        Duckles 67—792; Duckles 74—1101
A valuable chronological list of publications having at least one instrumental part—excluding lute music and dramatic music. The base volume was prepared under difficult conditions during and immediately after the War; consequently, many gaps and errors will be found in it; however, the 1968 supplement has accounted for most of these. Information provided includes bibliographical imprint, dedications and prefatory matter, names of pieces in each collection, library locations. Indexes of composers, dedicatees, authors of various textual items, publishers, printers, engravers, booksellers, titles, and captions.

0438   Upsala. Universitet. Bibliotek. **Catalogue critique et descriptif des imprimés de musique des XVIe et XVIIe siècles, conservés à la Bibliothèque de l'Université Royale d'Upsala; Par Rafael Mitjana** . . . Upsala: Impr. Almqvist Wiksell, 1911-51. 3v. ML136 U8 U5
        Duckles 67—1095; Duckles 74—1497
Only Volume I was by Mitjana; the other two volumes by Åke Davidsson. First two volumes list 456 editions in composer sequence within broad classes (religious music, secular music, dramatic, instrumental); bibliographic data is given, with locations in other libraries. The final volume arranges the entries in chronological order, from 1533 to 1698, and offers a composer index to the contents of collections—with all pieces by each composer under his name. (There is no index to titles.) This Upsala list is supplemented by Davidsson's inventory of early imprints in other Swedish libraries (0430).

0439   Vogel, Emil. **Bibliothek der gedruckten weltlichen Vocalmusik italiens aus den Jahren 1500-1700** . . . Berlin: A. Haack, 1892. 2v. Supplements in *Notes* 2 (1945) through 5 (1948), *passim*; by Alfred Einstein. (Reprint, with supplements—Hildesheim: Georg Olms, 1962. 2v.). ML120 I8 V8
        Duckles 67—803; Duckles 74—1110
Further supplementary material has appeared, to round out the addenda given by Einstein—who dealt only with collections having works by two or more composers:

        Hilmar, Ernst. "Ergänzungen zu Emil Vogels 'Bibliothek . . .',"
        Analecta musicologica 4 (1967), 154-206.
        Imprints by individual composers.

Hilmar, Ernst. "Weitere Ergänzungen . . . ," *Analecta musicologica* 5 (1968), 295-93.
Continues earlier supplement.

Bianconi, Lorenzo. "Weitere Ergänzungen . . . ," *Analecta musicologica* 9 (1970), 142-202.
Inventory of printed editions of madrigals and cantatas in Italian archives and libraries.

Wolfenbüttel. Herzog-August-Bibliothek. **Kataloge** . . .
See 0257. One of the greatest collections of early music, with German imprints strongly emphasized. Composer sequence, with anthologies and liturgical works by date. The composer list also cites works by each artist that appear in the collections of the next section. Chronological, name, title, and first-line indexes. Some entries after 1750 are found: the total range is from 1487 to 1826.

Many of the bibliographies and catalogs of early music appear to overlap; indeed, there is a good share of multiple coverage. But differences among these sources are worth noting, with regard to amount of information given and distinguishing formats or indexes. For example, there are numerous listings of printed editions by individual composers (Einzeldrucke): Eitner's *Quellen-Lexikon* (0187) and its successor RISM Series A (0419), various British Museum lists (0248, 0378, 0424), the *British Union Catalogue* (0426), inventories of the Brussels (0429) and Wolfenbüttel (0257) libraries, Sartori's Italian list (0437), etc. So the problem of locating pre-1800 material by given composers is not terribly difficult—and it gets easier as RISM moves ahead. But if the information search begins with a *title*, and the idea is to find the composer's name (or the date, or publisher, or other facts about the piece), only a few sources can be of much use: Brussels (0429), Sartori (0437, second volume), Wolfenbüttel (0257) and above all the *British Union Catalogue* (0426). Or suppose we are looking for early printed anthologies of music—RISM Series B is a comprehensive gathering. But notice that its sequencing of entries is chronological for pre-1700 entries and then by title for eighteenth century items. Suppose we need to know the names of early anthologies by genre (say, keyboard collections)? The old Becker *Tonwerke* (0421) may be the best answer, because of its classed arrangement. If the approach must be through the first line of a vocal text, consultation of the Eitner *Sammelwerke* (0420) or Huntington Library *Catalogue* (0433) may be germane. Hopefully the annotations given with all the early-music sources will indicate which are preferable from one access point or another.

LISTS OF 19th AND 20th CENTURY MUSIC

It may be well to remind the reader that the present volume, *Basic and Universal Sources*, generally excludes works that are specialized either by nationalistic limits or by narrow topical boundaries. As we come near to our own time, the number of universal bibliographies grows smaller; a function of the ever-climbing rate of musical publication in the world. (Consider that the U.S. copyright office registers some 80,000 musical works annually.) Attempts at bibliographic control necessarily become more restricted in their focus: they aim at gathering the titles of twentieth century violin sonatas, or of modern Swedish orchestral writing. These approaches are embodied in many sources to be presented in later volumes. A few important works of wide scope are given now.

0440   Altmann, Wilhelm. **Orchester-Literatur-Katalog: Verzeichnis von seit 1850 erschienenen Orchester-Werken** . . . Leipzig: F. E. C. Leuckart, 1926-36. (1st ed. 1919). 2v. Enlarged ed. (Reprint—Walluf bei Wiesbaden: Sändig, 1972. 2v. vi, 227p.; xvii, 187p.). ML128 O5 A5 Duckles 67—662; Duckles 74—875

A list of works for orchestra in various forms (suites, overtures, symphonies, concertos, etc.) published after 1850, to 1935. Includes miniature scores, arrangements; gives instrumentation and durations. Composer index. Buschkötter's *Handbuch* (0364) has some later entries.

0441   Deutscher Musikverleger-Verband. **Bonner Katalog. Verzeichnis der urheberrechtlich geschützten musikalischen Werke mit reversgebundenem Aufführungsmaterial.** Bonn: Musikhandel Verlagsgesellschaft, 1959. xi, 326p. ML145 D35 Duckles 67—619; Duckles 74—842

A composer list of music registered for international copyright. Some 13,000 titles, most of them twentieth century but also editions of earlier composers. Information: genre, duration, publisher; no dates. No title or other indexes. An imposing array of works, but not reliable as a measure of actual output by modern composers; e.g., 20 works listed by Samuel Barber, 40 by Arnold Bax, four by Leonard Bernstein, none by Ernst Levy. And many of the titles included are less than monumental—such as "Die Blume von Hawaii."

Documents du demi-siècle.
See 0107.

0442   Internationales Musikinstitut. **Internationales Musikinstitut Darmstadt: Informationszentrum für zeitgenössische Musik; Katalog der Abteilung Noten.** Darmstadt: Internationales Musikinstitut, 1966. Noten-Katalog Nachtrag 1967, 1967. ML113 I65 Duckles 67—883; Duckles 74—1224

A composer list of some 13,000 titles, primarily from the 1940s, 1950s, and early 1960s. Medium and publisher mentioned; no other information. This is a working catalog of the Musikinstitut, a lending library of contemporary scores.

Further sources of post-1800 titles are the other chronologies cited in Chapter 2, under "Chronologies," especially Gutknecht (0108), Lowe (0109), Schering (0111), and Slonimsky (0112); and many of the selective and critical lists in Chapter 4, under "Selective and Critical Guides," especially Buschkötter (0364), Daniels (0365), Dove (0366) and Fuchs (0367). Notice also the good nineteenth century coverage in certain library catalogs, particularly 0370 to 0373, 0382, and the Library of Congress group (0387 to 0389). The great compilations of Hofmeister (0258) will be cited again later under "Annual and Periodic Lists"; but they can well be brought forward here also. A massive listing of (principally) nineteenth century compositions was that of Pazdirek (0385).

The remarks volunteered after the preceding section (p. 114) need no review at this point; it is just as true of modern bibliography as of early bibliography that various approaches and information requirements are best served by some sources and least served by others. Comparison of the annotations should yield indications of the most useful beginnings for inquiries of diverse character.

THEMATIC INDEXES

A thematic index or catalog is a list of compositions with bits of their actual music attached; the music is usually the opening measures of the piece, but it may be the true theme. Ideally, a quote of the opening should be entitled an "incipit"; of course, in much early music the incipit is also the theme (e.g., in a fugue, or a classical minuet), but in later music a composition rarely begins with its theme. This lexicographical nicety notwithstanding, the generic term "thematic index"—or "thematic catalog"—has been universally accepted for a presentation of incipits and/or themes. This aspect of thematics is admirably discussed in Barry S. Brook's "A Tale of Thematic Catalogues," *Notes* 29-3 (March 1973), 407-415. Professor Brook also categorizes thematic indexes, with the following main types emerging: the table of contents of an edition; the guide to output of a composer; the inventory of a library; advertisements of publishers and firms; compilations of true themes; indexes serving as musicological documentation. More than 1,700 such catalogs have been identified by Professor Brook in 0443; only a selection of major, general, universal indexes is presented in the immediate volume, with others given place later according to their specializations.

0443   Brook, Barry S. **Thematic Catalogues in Music: An Annotated Bibliography; Including Printed, Manuscript, and In-Preparation Catalogues; Related Literature and Reviews; An Essay on the Definitions, History, Functions, Historiography, and Future of the Thematic Catalogue** ... Published under the sponsorship of the Music Library Association and RILM Abstracts of Music Literature. Hillsdale, N.Y.: Pendragon Press, 1972. (RILM Retrospectives, 1). xxxvi, 347p. ML113 B86
    Duckles 74–1839
    Supersedes *A Check List of Thematic Catalogues in Music* issued by the Music Library Association in 1953, and Brook's own *Queens College Supplement* ... of 1966. The main list is by composer, or by compiler for

eclectic catalogs, or by library for inventories of holdings. Incipits and themes covered. Thorough bibliographic descriptions. Index to names, subjects, genres, and titles; with library catalogs grouped by country and city.

For each of the following entries, references to "Brook numbers" are made, in addition to Duckles citations. Theme indexes first, then incipit indexes.

0444   Barlow, Harold, and Sam Morgenstern. **A Dictionary of Musical Themes** . . . New York: Crown, 1948; London: Williams and Norgate, 1949. xiii, 656p. ML128 I65 B3
        Duckles 67–279; Duckles 74–366; Brook 68
About 10,000 themes in composer sequence. Melodic line only, usually four to six measures; harmonization not indicated; tempo marking not given. Inclusion policy appears rather arbitrary, at least by today's priorities; e.g., only two Bartók quartets are found, two themes from Ives, but 27 themes by Sarasate and 26 by Anton Rubinstein. Nevertheless useful for jogging the memory on standard repertoire. A good title index, and a foolish attempt to index the tunes themselves in a clumsy alphabetic notation. An Italian translation was issued under the editorship of H. Dahnk: *Dizionario dei temi musicali* (Milano: Sormani, 1955). Instrumental themes are the province of 0444; vocal themes appear in its companion volume:

0445   Barlow, Harold, and Sam Morgenstern. **A Dictionary of Opera and Song Themes, Including Cantatas, Oratorios, Lieder, and Art Songs**. New York: Crown, 1966. vi, 547p. ML128 V7 B3
        Duckles 67–280; Duckles 74–367; Brook 69
This is a reprint of *A Dictionary of Vocal Themes* (Crown, 1950), unchanged except for the title. It covers some 8,000 themes, with a good presentation of the standard opera arias and best-known nineteenth century art songs; shares the unbalanced selection policy of 0444. Good title index, useful for identifying composers of vocal pieces even if the theme itself is not needed. Short melodic extracts, unharmonized, without tempo markings; text of each song or aria printed under the notes. The same sort of alpha-notation index as that of 0444.

0446   Burrows, Raymond, and Bessie Carroll Redmond. **Concerto Themes**. New York: Simon and Schuster, 1951. xxxviii, 296p. ML128 O5 B8
        Duckles 67–282; Duckles 74–369; Brook 208
Main themes of 144 concertos, for various instruments, from Bach to Addinsell. A sensible selection, sensibly presented—with harmonization, tempo markings, cues to instrumentation, dates and publishers, and citations of analyses or program notes. Title index, plus an interesting list of works in each key.

0447   Burrows, Raymond, and Bessie Carroll Redmond. **Symphony Themes**. New York: Simon and Schuster, 1942. 295p. MT125 B87 S9
        Duckles 67–283; Duckles 74–370; Brook 207

Displays themes from 100 symphonies, in the manner of 0446. Standard traditional repertoire well represented, along with a number of efforts no longer on the charts. Citations to analyses and program notes, dates, and publishers. Useful: durations, taken from New York Philharmonic or NBC Symphony performances; in some cases from composer recommendations. Full instrumentation also given, and grouping of works by key.

0448   LaRue, Jan. **Union Thematic Catalogue of Concertos**. 1959— . (index cards).
      Brook 713
This and the following item are unpublished files, included here— despite their relative inaccessibility—for their scope and scholarly attributes. The concerto index gives some 8,000 entries for works composed between 1740 and 1810, arranged by composer with tune index. A "disputed paternity" file is under way (see 0449).

0449   LaRue, Jan. **Union Thematic Catalogue of 18th-Century Symphonies**. 1954— . (index cards).
      Brook 712
Between 12,000 and 13,000 works are covered, in composer array. Each composer card offers thematic and background material, including library and catalog sources. "Locator" cards arranged "by key, mode, and time signature, then according to the principle of least melodic motion from the initial pitch" (Brook). About 650 "disputed paternity" cards have resulted from discovery, by Professor LaRue, that certain works have been credited to more than one composer. This approach has enabled LaRue to make some judgments on authorship of works that had been variously attributed.

0450   Schiegl, Hermann, und Ernst Schwarzmaier. **Themensammlung musikalischer Meisterwerke**. Heft 1: Symphonische Musik der Klassik. 4. Auflage. Frankfurt am Main: M. Diesterweg, 1967. Heft 2: Symphonische Musik der Romantik. 2. Auflage. Frankfurt am Main: M. Diesterweg, 1967. (1st ed. Heft 1, 1959; Heft 2, 1964). ML113 S39
      Brook 1163
Major works of Gluck, Haydn, Mozart, Beethoven, Schubert, Weber, Schumann, Brahms, Bruckner, Dvorak, Tchaikovsky, and Wagner. Long thematic quotations, with tempo markings, harmonization, and instrumentation indicated. Basis for structural analysis of each work is provided by an interesting digest of the different themes and recurrences of each movement.

The remaining items are catalogs of incipits.

0451   Eulenburg, Ernst, *firm*. **Thematisches Verzeichnis**. 4. Ausgabe. Leipzig: Eulenburg, 19— . (1st ed. 1901?). 54p. ML145 E87
      Brook 362c

Original edition gave incipits for choral and orchestral works, concertos, chamber music, and keyboard works. This fourth edition omits the keyboard section. Incipits are very brief, often leaving the actual theme incomplete; chords are given. Composers include Bach, Beethoven, Brahms, Dvořák, Handel, Haydn, Liszt, Mendelssohn, Mozart, Schubert, Schumann, and Tchaikovsky. Brook remarks that the Eulenburg first edition is virtually the same as:

> Chester, J. and W., Ltd. **Reference Book of Miniature Scores with Thematic List of the Symphonies and Chamber Music Works of the Great Masters**. Ed. Henry J. Wood. London: Chester, 1924.
> Brook 237

0452 Rutová, Milada. [**Waldstein-Doksy Music Collection: Thematic Catalogue**]. Ph.D. dissertation, Praha, Charles University, 1971. 600, 170p.
Brook 989
English title from Brook. Covers chamber and orchestral works from 1750 to 1800, in the Hudební oddělení národního Musea, Praha (Prague). There are 1,500 incipits from all the masters and hundreds of lesser-known composers.

0453 Stockholm. Kungliga Musikaliska Akademiens Bibliothek. [**Card catalogue now consisting of 36,000 incipits . . . 1968– .**]
Brook 1253
Title supplied by Brook. A mammoth union list of several thematic sources: Swedish RISM manuscript entries, and (so far) 39 published compilations of incipits. Indexes to individual composers searched and melodies interfiled: about 30, including Corelli, Haydn, Mozart, Telemann, Vivaldi. Publishers' incipit catalogs (e.g., *The Breitkopf Thematic Catalogue*, 0423), and thematics from various "monuments" and anthologies.

Sources cited earlier with thematic/incipit indexes include: Eitner (0187), New York Public Library (0233), Paris Bibliothèque National (0253), Llorens (0410), Ludwig (0412), RISM (0419), Breitkopf (0423), and Paris Conservatoire (0436).

ANNUAL AND PERIODIC LISTS

Most of the sources for a continuing account of publication for musical scores have already been cited: *Bibliographie de la France* (0271), *Bibliographie musicale française* (0272), *Bibliografia nazionale italiana* (0277), *Bolletino delle pubblicazioni italiane* (0276), *British Catalogue of Music* (0263), *Deutsche Musikbibliographie* (and *Jahresverzeichnis*) (0258), and the Library of Congress *Music and Phonorecords* (0387). Only the last-named is truly international; but we must remember that it lists materials only when cataloging has taken place, some time after publication.

A few other sources for newly published musical editions follow.

0454 **Letopis' muzykal'noi literatury** [Chronicle of Musical Literature], 1931-1941, 1945– . Moskva: Izd-vo Vsesoiuznoi Knizhnoi Palaty, 1931-41, 1945– . (quarterly). ML120 R8 N6
    Duckles 67–650; Duckles 74–832
Lists, by genre, music published in Soviet countries and some Western materials that are acquired by the All-Union Book Chamber. Composer index; title and first-line indexes annually. Descriptive notes on each entry, with contents identified in multiple works.

0455 **Musikbibliographischer Dienst.** Berlin: Deutscher Büchereiverband, Arbeitsstelle für das Büchereiwesen, 1969/70– . (bimonthly, annual cumulation).
    Duckles 74–828
International lists of serious music; about 1,500 titles per year; began in classed order with composer index, then changed to the opposite plan. Also index to publishers and authors of texts for vocal pieces. Bibliographic descriptions. This is a companion publication to 0291.

Several journals carry notices of new music issues. *Fontes* has been mentioned (0432); others are the *Journal of the American Musicological Society*, 1948– , and *Notes* (0285). In *Musical Quarterly* (0283) there is an interesting feature, "Current Chronicle," which offers reviews of new music performances.

MISCELLANEOUS LISTS

Lists of music are everywhere. We have already seen hundreds of sources in the preceding sections that offer some kind of list: e.g., in the biographical works the output of a composer is often given; in the encyclopedic works the compositions of a certain type or nationality will be mentioned—with varying degrees of completeness. Let us here select some items for restatement because of their special features. Berkowitz (0159), Leipoldt (0166), and Quarry (0167) are very helpful identifiers of titles, including nickname-titles and other popular unofficial designations for musical pieces. The index in Prieberg (0201) is a fine commencement for tracking contemporary titles.

Discographies—in the following unit—are also valuable as lists of music, and for identifying obscure compositions.

Specialized lists (of songs, music for certain instruments, etc.) are covered in Volume 3.

CHAPTER 6

GENERAL DISCOGRAPHIES

A "bibliography" is a list of books or, by extension, a list of writings; a "discography" is a list of discs or, by comparable extension, a list of recordings in any format. While bibliography is ancient, discography is a creation of our own century, and it may be viewed as an emerging science that is not fully structured or conceptualized. Gordon Stevenson has sought out some "solid theoretical underpinnings" in a remarkably perceptive study: "Discography: Scientific, Analytical, Historical and Systematic," pp. 101-135 of:

0456 **Trends in Archival and Reference Collections of Recorded Sound.**
Gordon Stevenson, issue editor. *Library Trends*, 21/1 (July 1972).
Eight articles, including the one by Stevenson already mentioned, and one by Donald Robbins to be cited later (in the section "Annual and Periodic Discographies"). All the contributions are useful, though most of the emphasis is on the archival rather than the biblio-discographical aspects of the topic.

In addition to a theory, discography has been in need of order. "An urgent desideratum," wrote Stevenson in the article just cited, "is a bibliography of discographies." The recent effort of David Cooper (0458) offers a partial response to that call, and suggests the formidable stature already attained by the new discographical art: he identifies 1,820 discographies issued between 1962 and 1972. Bibliographic control over recordings is at a stage of development comparable to that for published scores 100 years ago. We have seen our discographic Beckers and Eitners, those who have tried to sweep the recording horizon and list whatever they saw (e.g., WERM, 0463). It is now a time for more narrow and intensive viewpoints: inventories of production by individual manufacturers, of issues by certain performers, or in certain forms and styles. Our Pazdirek (0385) is Schwann (0477); our RISM (0419) will have to wait another generation.

In the present work, most discographies are dispersed by subject. For this volume we have selected only a small number, which may represent the widest range of current interest. They deal primarily with so-called classical and semi-classical music; jazz and pop are treated in Volume 3.

BIBLIOGRAPHIES OF DISCOGRAPHIES

Lists of record lists are rather scarce. Guides to reference sources usually name some discographies; there are 77 citations in Duckles (0216).

Discographies are sometimes listed under that heading in the Library of Congress *Subjects* (0236); other times they are under more specific topics. But there are just two attempts to confront the field comprehensively.

0457   Bruun, C. L., and J. Gray. "A Bibliography of Discographies." *Recorded Sound*, 1/7 (1962), 206-213. ML5 R188
        About 450 entries. Cylinder recordings included. Excludes jazz and pop.

0458   Cooper, David E. **International Bibliography of Discographies: Classical Music, and Jazz and Blues, 1962-1972; A Reference Book for Record Collectors, Dealers, and Libraries.** Littleton, Colo.: Libraries Unlimited, [announced for 1975]. (Keys to Music Bibliography, No. 2).
        Contains 1,908 entries, of which 1,155 are for serious music, 665 for jazz and blues, and 88 national bibliographies or review sources. Arranged by subject, composer, performer; with indexing by author and title. Thorough and accurate, with bibliographic detail but no annotations. Based on the author's *A Bibliography of Discographies . . . 1962-1971* (Master's Research Paper, Kent State University, School of Library Science, 1973).

    Another valuable survey is that of Robbins (0456).

SELECTIVE AND CRITICAL LISTS

    Probably the earliest compilers of "best records" books were David Hall (*The Record Book . . .* New York: Smith and Durrell, 1940) and Irving Kolodin (*A Guide to Recorded Music.* Garden City, N.Y.: Doubleday, 1941). Each carried his work through three editions, the last in each case being issued in 1950—when the LP avalanche began. The style of critical commentary on recording techniques and performer interpretation is found today in several solid books.

0459   De Nys, Carl. **La Discothèque idéale.** Rev. ed. Paris: Éditions Universitaires, 1973. (1st ed. 1970). 443p. (La Bibliothèque Idéale). ML156.2 D587
        Classed arrangement of preferred performances, with comments. European and American discs included. Composer/artist indexes.

0460   Lory, Jacques. **Guide des disques: L'Aventure de la musique occidentale, du chant grégorien à la musique électronique** . . . 3d éd. Paris: Buchet-Chastel, 1971. (1st ed. 1967). xxvii, 416p. ML156.2 L63
        About 2,500 recordings—mostly LP but with some 78 rpm—in historical order. Comments on the musical background of each period, and on the discs. A good selection of performances, primarily drawn from 40 European and American labels.

0461   **The Stereo Record Guide**. Ed. Edward Greenfield *et al*. Blackpool:
Long-Playing Record Library, Ltd., 1960– .
Duckles 67–1271; Duckles 74–1754; Winchell 67–BH137
Volume 8, 1972. First two volumes retrospective: reviewed all
stereo records issued to the end of 1960. Later volumes evaluate current
releases, in composer order. Spoken records included; some popular. Symbols
to indicate preferences, long commentaries comparing performances. Volumes 5 and 6 in a sense supersede the preceding: they present a "current
reassessment" of the stereo scene—evaluating new issues and referring back to
critiques for earlier issues in the prior volumes. No performer index; however,
recital and concert discs are grouped under names of performers.

GENERAL LISTS

No comprehensive gathering of LP titles has been attempted so far,
but the old 78 rpm's did receive a respectable inventory.

0462   Gramophone Shop, Inc., *New York*. **The Gramophone Shop
Encyclopedia of Recorded Music**. 3d ed., Robert H. Reid, super-
vising ed. New York: Crown, 1948. (1st ed. 1936; comp. by R. D.
Darrell. 2d ed. 1942; George C. Leslie, supervising ed. Publisher
varies). xii, 639p. (Reprint—Westport, Conn.: Greenwood Press,
1970). ML156 G83
Duckles 67–1257; Duckles 74–1736
Compiles "all listings of serious music currently to be found in the
catalogues of the world's record manufacturers . . ."; i.e., it is an in-print list.
Ergo, each edition has some items not in the others. Covers 66 labels from
Europe (including USSR) and America. Composer arrangement; some topical
groups. Useful performer index.

0463   Clough, Francis F., and G. J. Cuming. **The World's Encyclopaedia of
Recorded Music**. London: Sidgwick and Jackson, 1952. xviii, 890p.
First Supplement (April 1950—May/June 1951) bound in. Second
Supplement (1951-52), London: Sidgwick and Jackson, 1952. 262p.
Third Supplement (1953-55), London: Sidgwick and Jackson, 1957.
564p. (Reprint—Westport, Conn.: Greenwood Press, 1970). 3v.
ML156.2 C6
Duckles 67–1256; Duckles 74–1735; Winchell 67–BH127; ARBA
72–1133
Based on 0462. Aims to identify all recordings of "permanent
music." Composer order (subarranged by genre and title), with a title
sequence for anthologies. Artist, label and number, speed, some information
on reissues; but year of first issue not given. Base volume displays some
40,000 items on more than 300 labels, from 1925 to 1951. Third Supplement
has errata and addenda for the preceding volumes. Lack of a performer index
here makes reference to 0462 necessary for that kind of search; in other
respects WERM may be said to supersede it.

0464   RAI–Radiotelevisione Italiana. Direzione Programmi Radio. Disco-
           teca Centrale. **Catalogo della discoteca storica**. 1a serie. Roma:
           RAI–Radiotelevisione Italiana, Servizio Archivi, 1969. 3v. ML156.2
           R24 C4
           A very informative catalog of the 78-rpm collection, consisting of
about 4,000 discs: 6,906 titles by 3,281 performers. Arranged in sections
(opera, chamber music, film, folk, jazz, spoken, etc.), and by composer
within sections–except that pop records are by title. Label information
provided. Names of all performers on pop/jazz recordings, with their
instruments–even for "big bands."

        And one of the largest general lists is the Library of Congress *Music,
Books on Music, and Sound Recordings* (0387).

MANUFACTURER LISTS

        More than a thousand "labels"–of disc and tape manufacturers–are
found in current issues of the *Schwann Record and Tape Guide* (0477). All
but a handful of those companies have entered the field during the LP
era–that is, over the past 25 years. Most companies issue occasional sales lists
of their output, but bibliographic catalogs–with full data on recording dates,
issue dates, matrix numbers, re-issues, performers, etc.–are available only for
a few firms and for limited periods. Indeed, such bibliographies, as opposed
to sales lists, are typically the work of independent researchers, rather than of
the companies themselves. Most effort of this kind has been directed toward
early recordings, on cylinders and discs, issued by certain companies. A
particularly fine specimen is this one, for RCA Victor:

0465   Rust, Brian A. **The Victor Master Book**. Vol. 2 (1925-36). Stanhope,
           N.J.: W. C. Allen, 1970. 776p. ML156 V423 R92
           Victor Black Label and Bluebird (except ethnic). Arranged in date
order by label. Identifies all performers with full instrumentation of
orchestras and bands. Indexes by matrix number, title, and performer. Vol. 1
in preparation.

        A companion inventory is:

0466   Smolian, Steven. "Da Capo." *American Record Guide*, 30 (May
           1964), 892-95; (June 1964), 1002-1004; (July 1964), 1956-58; 31
           (September 1964), 82-84; (October 1964), 165-67; (November
           1964), 271-73; (February 1965), 582-83; (April 1965), 763-65.
           A complete numerical list of RCA Victor Red Seal albums.

        The company itself, The "Victor Talking Machine Company"
according to Library of Congress entries, has produced many in-print
catalogs, catalogs of "educational" records, withdrawn records, numerical
lists, alphabetical lists, etc. We do not endeavor here to cite all such works,
which may be readily located through Cooper (0458) and/or the "Music–

Discography–Catalogs" section of any volume of L.C.'s *Books: Subjects* (0236). Similar material for other companies can be found in those sources. Edison cylinder lists are covered in the following section.

LISTS OF EARLY RECORDINGS

Many sources already described give attention to pioneer recordings; but these that follow are concentrated efforts to catalog the entire pioneer repertoire from one viewpoint or another. Thomas Edison made his first talking cylinder (of himself reciting "Mary had a little lamb") in 1877; cylinders were soon marketed commercially. Disc recordings began to flow in the 1890s, and of course drove cylinders out of the field. The piano roll was an alternative form that was popular in the 1920s and 1930s (and that is still available).

This item considers both discs and cylinders:

0467   Girard, Victor, and Harold M. Barnes. **Vertical-Cut Cylinders and Discs: A Catalogue of All "Hill-and-Dale" Recordings of Serious Worth Made and Issued between 1897-1932 Circa**. London: British Institute of Recorded Sound, 1964. xxxviii, 196p. Corrected reprint, 1971. ML155 S2 G57
        Duckles 67–1275; Duckles 74–1760

Performer lists of issues, grouped in vocal, speech, opera, and instrumental sections.

The next two sources deal with cylinders only:

0468   Koenigsberg, Allen. **Edison Cylinder Records, 1889-1912**. New York: Stellar Productions, 1969. 159p. ML155.59 K64
        Duckles 74–1763; ARBA 71–1257

Arranged by artist. Release dates and other information; historical commentary. Reproductions of early catalogs.

0469   Walsh, J. "A March, 1901, Catalog of Edison 'Concert' Cylinders." *Hobbies*, 71 (November 1966), 37-38+; (December 1966), 37-38; (January 1967), 37.

A carefully described presentation of the contents of this sales catalog, which included instrumentalists, singers, a chimes number, a brass quartet, and a whistler.

These are the principal inventories of early discs. Since the recording techniques of the pioneer period favored reproduction of the singing voice, much of this output is vocal.

0470   Bauer, Robert. **The New Catalogue of Historical Records, 1898-1908/09**. 2d ed. London: Sidgwick and Jackson, 1947. (1st ed. 1937). 494p. ML156 B33
        Duckles 67–1272; Duckles 74–1756; Winchell 67–BH126

Endeavors to list recordings on lateral-cut discs by "all internationally famous opera and concert singers." Covers these labels: Berliner

Gramophone, Gramophone, Typewriter, Gramophone Co. Ltd., International Zonophone, Columbia, Victor, Fonotipia, and Odeon. Arranged by singer, and label sequence numbers. Supplementary lists: 25 instrumentalists (e.g., Sarasate, Grieg, Joachim) and eight speakers (e.g., Sarah Bernhardt). Also a list of complete operas: Aida, Fledermaus, Carmen, Faust, and Tannhäuser. Estimated 1,920 artists in all. Unfortunately, information given about the actual discs is very slight.

0471   Bennett, John Reginald. **Voices of the Past: Vocal Recordings, 1898-1925**. Lingfield, Surrey: Oakwood, 1956– . ML156.4 V7 B45
Duckles 67–1273; Duckles 74–1766
Surveys the output of the Gramophone Company and affiliates. Published to date:

V. 1: **The English Catalogues**. 1957.

V. 2: **The Italian Catalogues**. 1958.

V. 3: **Dischi Fonotipia**. 1964?

V. 4 and V. 6: **International Red Label Catalogue of DB and DA "His Master's Voice" Recordings, 1924-1956**. 1961, 1963.

V. 5: **HMV Black Label Catalogue. The Gramophone Company D and E Series**. 1960.

V. 7: **The German Catalogues**. 1967.

V. 8: **The Columbia Catalogue English Celebrity Issues**. 1972.

V. 9: **The French Catalogues**. 1971?

0472   Celletti, Rodolfo. **Le Grandi Voci. Dizionario critico-biografico dei cantanti con discografia operistica**. Roma: Istituto per la Collaborazione Culturale, 1964. xiv, 1p., 1044 cols., 1p. ML400 C44
Duckles 67–64; Duckles 74–84; Winchell 67–1BH25
Biographical information on some 250 famous opera singers, including some contemporaries, with comprehensive discographies. Section on complete and selective opera recordings. 48 portraits.

0473   Moses, Julian Morton. **Collectors' Guide to American Recordings, 1895-1925**. New York: American Record Collectors Exchange, 1949. 199p. ML156.2 M67
Duckles 67–1277; Duckles 74–1765; Winchell 67–BH131
Brief biographical information on about 235 performers, with more than 7,000 recordings made by them. Serial or matrix numbers; index by opera and instruments. Note also the next item.

0474   Moses, Julian Morton. **Price Guide to Collectors' Records**. New York: American Record Collectors Exchange, 1967. (1st ed. 1952). 28p. ML156.2 M677

Duckles 74—1765; Duckles 74—1765
Gives approximate market value of discs listed in 0473.

Here are two interesting catalogs of piano rolls:

0475   Aeolian Company, New York. **Duo-Art Piano Music: A Classified Catalog of Interpretations of the World's Best Music Recorded by More than Two Hundred and Fifty Pianists for the Duo-Art Reproducing Piano.** New York: The Aeolian Company, 1927. 480p.
ML128 P3 A376
Composer and performer lists.

0476   **Library of Welte-Mignon Music Records.** 2d ed.? New York: DeLuxe Reproducing Roll Corp., 1927. (A 1st ed. 1924 listed in *National Union Catalog*). 323p.
Performances by famous pianists on a device called the Vorsetzer, which punched their interpretations into rolls. Busoni, Ganz, Grieg, Glazunov, Leschetizky, Saint-Saëns, etc. Arranged by pianists, with composer and title indexes.

ANNUAL AND PERIODIC DISCOGRAPHIES

More than 5,000 new LP discs are released every year, and around 50,000 discs are currently "in print." Despite this imposing volume of production, discographic control over new issues is good—with certain limitations. Most commercially sold recordings from Europe or North America will be listed in *Schwann* (0477) or one of the other major catalogs (0478-0481). Furthermore, there is access to individual pieces on anthology discs ("albums," as the common parlance terms them), whether these are pop songs or specific Chopin mazurkas; this angle of approach—the "analytic"—is found in the Gramophone *Classical*, Bielefelder (0480), *One-Spot* (0482), and *Phonolog* (0483). A search via performer name can be carried out through all the sources mentioned in this section. Limitations of these sources are: non-cumulation, and lack of subject approach. Since all the services discussed below are devoted to catching the immediate scene, they list only currently in-print material (dropping "cut-outs" to make room for new releases)—so we need to consult all issues to make a comprehensive discography of, say, the Schubert Unfinished, or of Glenn Gould performances. (Of course, that sort of task is precisely the purpose of items in the preceding sections.) The other limitation is lack of approach to discs and tapes by musical form or subject or instrument. We are unable to use these sources to find—except through a page-by-page search—what recent recordings of psalm settings there are, or what fugues; we cannot locate conveniently the new trumpet or string trio recordings, or vocal duets.

Still, the state of the art is much more advanced in this relatively new field than it is for printed music itself. A good overview of the present scene is given by Donald C. Robbins in an article found in 0456: "Current Resources for the Bibliographic Control of Sound Recordings.' (pp. 136-46).

This is the pioneer guide to LP recordings, which has become the most widely known and used catalog of disc and tape music:

0477   **Schwann Record and Tape Guide**. Boston: W. Schwann, Inc., 1949– . (monthly for *Schwann-1*; semiannual for *Schwann-2*). ML156.2 S385
        Duckles 67–1300; Duckles 74–1802; Winchell 67–BH136; ARBA 72–1128+

Title and format vary. First issue, October 1949, entitled *Long Playing Record Catalog*; it carried 674 discs by eleven companies (Allegro, Artist, Capitol, Cetra-Soria, Columbia, Concert Hall, Decca, London, Mercury, Polydor and Vox—note that Victor was not yet producing LP discs, having decided to promote 45 rpm). In 1973, discs by more than 800 companies are listed, as well as tapes by another 300 companies; each issue enumerates some 45,000 items. The object of these catalogs has always been to itemize recordings currently on sale by their manufacturers; thus, each monthly *Schwann* presents both old and new discs, intermingled. "New listings" are offered in separate sections, however, before being interfiled in the following month. Information contained in the "New listing" is more extensive than in the later entries for a given disc (e.g., contents of anthology records are noted) and reference back to dates of a disc's appearance as a "new" are included in all later citations. Basic arrangement is by composer for serious music, by performer for popular; miscellaneous collections are separately grouped. Information: composer dates, title and opus number (also thematic numbers—Köchel, Schmieder, Fanna, etc.), performer, language, other works on disc, label, number, price.

The foregoing was a description of the monthly *Schwann* as it has appeared since 1949. Irregular "supplementary" catalogs were also issued from time to time, covering children's records, international folk music, and certain other categories not in the monthly catalog. In 1972, the overall format was stabilized with the traditional monthly issue given the name *Schwann-1*, and a semiannual supplement given the name *Schwann-2*. The semiannual contains monaural discs, educational, spoken, religious, international folk and popular, popular more than two years old, and a few other categories. Every few years, Schwann has published an *Artist Issue*, which arranges the current in-print serious music discs by performer; the most recent of these came out in 1970.

A special *Children's Record and Tape Guide* is issued each year before Christmas. A recent number carried some 1,500 recordings, disc and tape, mostly in title sequence.

Schwann's coverage of serious music is excellent and generally accurate, for discs; however, tape listings are less complete than those in *Harrison* (0479). And popular/jazz material is more thoroughly and conveniently presented in *One-Spot* and *Phonolog* (0480 and 0481). The following item duplicates much of *Schwann-1*, but it does have some useful features not found therein:

0478   The Gramophone. **Classical Record Catalogue**. Harrow, Middlesex: General Gramophone Publications, Ltd., 1953– . (quarterly). ML156.2 G67

Title and imprint vary. Issued by the publisher of *The Gramophone*, a journal devoted to reviews of records and audio equipment. Lists LP discs, tape cassettes and cartridges generally available in Great Britain. Basic arrangement by composer, with works presented by category (orchestral, chamber, instrumental, vocal, stage) under each name. A valuable feature, not found in *Schwann*, is inclusion of titles that appear on anthology recordings; thus, each piece of a violin recital record is located in its composer list. Another useful fact is the citation to whatever review may have been printed in *The Gramophone*. Finally, it is convenient to find all inclusions grouped by artist as well as by composer. Probably around 30,000 records in each issue—fewer than *Schwann* offers, but with many compositions given that *Schwann* does not have. The two must be used together for best coverage. Also by the same publisher: *Popular Record Catalogue* (quarterly) and *Spoken Word and Miscellaneous Catalogue* (annual); these correspond in scope to *Schwann-2*.

Various countries produce periodic catalogs that emphasize their national disc producers, and that may offer many titles not to be found in *Schwann* or the Gramophone set. Catalogs of this sort will be cited in Volume 2. A convenient compilation of recordings offered on about a hundred labels from 19 countries is the Peters sales list:

0479   **Imported Records and Tapes**. New York: Peters International, Inc., 1971– ?.
Lists some 3,000 items. A classical section, of 1,000 items, is available separately. Peters is U.S. agent for many companies whose output is not usually found in general trade catalogs (Fung Hang, from Hong Kong; Talisman, from Ireland; Splash, from Italy; Toshiba, from Japan; Minos, from Greece; etc.). This catalog is illustrated with small photos of record jackets—under which content information is given. Composer and artist lists follow. Tapes are treated similarly in a second part.

Probably the most important catalog from the continent is German:

0480   **Katalog der Schallplatten klassischer Musik**. Bielefeld: Bielefelder Verlagsanstalt KG, 1953– . (semiannual).
Covers about 75 companies. Composer arrangement, with analytic treatment of composite recordings. A comparison made by Robbins (0456) shows that more than half the items in this *Katalog* are not found in *Schwann* (0477). Bielefelder has separate catalogs for spoken and pop records.

This is the principal current compilation of titles on tape:

0481   **The Harrison Tape Catalog**. New York: Weiss Publishing Corp., 1953– . (bimonthly). ML156.2 H37
Title, imprint and frequency vary. Each issue now presents some 20,000 (estimated) tapes in all formats—open reel, 4-track, 8-track, cassette. All categories of material: pop, folk, jazz, "classical," religious, spoken,

children's, language, humor, etc. Minimal information (no contents of anthologies, and no individual listings of titles in them), frequent errors. More entries than *Schwann*, but the latter is more reliable.

Finally, there are two rather remarkable commercial services that proffer the most updated information about current recordings.

0482 **One-Spot [Guides].** Mt. Prospect, Ill.: One-Spot Publishing Division, Trade Service Publications, Inc. ML156.2 O5

A complex of lists and bulletins that cover the recording situation from the dealer viewpoint. Monthly title and artist guides give access to individual pieces on anthology discs; weekly "new release reporters" fill the intervals. A numerical index comes out monthly: it gives contents of albums in manufacturer-number sequence (covering 140 classical and popular labels); this item, which is looseleaf, is updated by replacement pages every two weeks. Trade Services Publications also issues *List-o-Tapes*, a looseleaf catalog of "50,000 listings [as described in a 1972 ad] kept up to date with weekly inserts." Unfortunately, a merger of One-Spot Publishers with Trade Services Publications seems to have led to the 1970 demise of the monthly classical guide. Coverage of serious music continues in the other Trade Services bibliography:

0483 **Phonolog.** Los Angeles: Trade Services Publications, Inc., 1948– .

This is a looseleaf service, which offers the subscriber a large base volume and replacement pages several times a week to bring information up to date. Serious music, pop, jazz, folk; singles, anthologies; discs, cassettes, tapes—more than 500 labels covered. All works by any performer (if in print) are listed—whether singles or pieces from composite "albums." All pieces can be found by title, and classical compositions by composer. Titles given in various languages as appropriate, to facilitate access (e.g., opera arias). Topical groupings of all sorts: marches, Latin American, polkas, etc.

Another service of this type is *Recordaid*, which covers classical and popular music on discs and tapes (Philadelphia: Recordaid, Inc., 1943– ; quarterly).

REVIEWS OF RECORDINGS

Items 0459 to 0461 offer retrospective judgments on recordings; the following sources are concerned with evaluation of new releases. They are a strong group, these people who review new records: by and large they are very well informed on past performances and on the music they listen to (a more reassuring panorama of ability and taste than we can attach to book reviewers as a class). Their critiques are published in a great many periodicals, of which the following are most often cited: *American Recorder, American Record Guide, Audio, Gramophone, Harper's, High Fidelity, London Sunday Times, Monthly Letter, New Records, New York Times, Opera, Opera News,*

Pan Pipes, *Previews* (media offshoot of *Library Journal*, which formerly carried recording reviews), *Saturday Review*, *Stereo Review*. Anyone who wishes to compare several reviews of a given recording will benefit from consulting one of the two current indexes:

0484 "Index to Record Reviews; with Symbols Indicating Opinions of Reviewers," compiled and edited by Kurtz Myers, in *Notes; the Quarterly Journal of the Music Library Association*. 2d series. 1948– . (quarterly).

Duckles 67–1298; Duckles 74–1800; Winchell 67–BH138

This valuable feature has appeared regularly in *Notes* since 1948, under the reliable direction of Mr. Myers. The December 1973 issue cites reviews in 16 periodicals (virtually the same titles as those mentioned above), with discs grouped by composer or–for composite discs–by manufacturer. There are composer cross-references from the first to the second section. The discs are bibliographically described, and then all reviews are listed (periodical only, not the reviewer's name) with signs to indicate the critic's opinion: excellent, adequate, inadequate, and a special designation for mechanical faults discerned. Unusually long or noteworthy reviews are also marked. About 250 discs reviewed in December 1973. Lack of cumulative indexing is a serious handicap to the user of this otherwise splendid service. There was one cumulation (0487) long ago.

0485 Maleady, Antoinette. **Record and Tape Reviews Index–1971; Record and Tape Reviews Index–1972**. Metuchen, N.J.: Scarecrow Press, 1972, 1973. v, 234p.; x, 510p. ML156.9 M28

Duckles 74–1811

Planned as an annual publication. Cites reviews of serious music and spoken recordings, disc and tape, which appeared in 16 (volume for 1971) or 18 (1972) periodicals–about the same titles that were mentioned in the introduction to this section. Composer arranged, with anthology albums by manufacturer. Performer index initiated with 1972 volume; also indication of reviewer opinion. See also 0489.

The next title is a useful gathering of reviews, made once a year from one of the leading journals.

0486 High Fidelity. **Records in Review, 1955–** . Great Barrington, Mass.: Wyeth Press, 1955– . (annual). ML156.9 H5

Duckles 67–1297; Duckles 74–1748; Winchell 67–BH141; ARBA 70–II, 28; ARBA 72–1126/27; ARBA 73–1035

These are the reviews themselves, not simply citations to them. They are taken from *High Fidelity*, which means that they are long, critical, signed commentaries. Arrangement by composer, with composites by type of music, artist, or album title; cross references in the composer section to items in the composite section. There is also a performer index. "Classical and semi-classical" music only.

These two guides to older reviews will be of occasional use:

0487   Myers, Kurtz. **Record Ratings: The Music Library Association's Index of Record Reviews.** Ed. by Richard S. Hill. New York: Crown, 1956. viii, 440p. ML156.9 M9
   Duckles 67–1259; Duckles 74–1738; Winchell 67–BH139
   Cumulates 0484 from 1948, following same format as the original quarterly issues. A performer index was prepared for the cumulation. Total periodicals cited: 28, of which 24 are American, three British, and one French.

0488   **Polart Index to Record Reviews, 1960-67.** Detroit: Polart, 1961-68. (annual). ML156.9 P64
   Duckles 67–1299; Duckles 74–1801; Winchell 67–BH140
   Citations to reviews in 14 periodicals. Included reviews of tapes beginning 1961. Arranged by composer, with composites separated. No information about the reviews or the opinions expressed, except for 1965, when length of the critique was indicated. Some pop/jazz items included. No indexes.

Sources for popular music are considered in Volume 3 of the present work; however, the next item should be mentioned as a companion publication to 0485:

0489   Armitage, Andrew D., and Dean Tudor. **Annual Index to Popular Music Record Reviews 1972.** Metuchen, N.J.: Scarecrow Press, 1973. 467p.
   ARBA 74–1131
   First issue of a planned yearly series. Cites all published reviews of LP discs (and tapes, if *Schwann* or *Harrison* lists them) in 35 English-language journals. Divided into 12 sections: rock, country, jazz, blues, etc., then by performer or anthology title. Indication of reviewer opinion given. This volume offers citations to 7,307 reviews for 3,679 recordings.

JAZZ–IN BRIEF

Volume 3 will give detailed attention to the sources of information for jazz, including relevant discographical works. However, it may be appropriate to identify here some of the major reference materials of the field. No descriptive commentaries are made at this time.
   The first three are bibliographic approaches to discography.

0490   Allen, Walter C. **Studies in Jazz Discography I. Proceedings of the First and Second Annual Conferences on Discographical Research, 1968-1969, and of the Conference on the Preservation and Extension of the Jazz Heritage, 1969.** New Brunswick, N.J.: Rutgers University, Institute of Jazz Studies, 1971.
   Duckles 74–1767

0491   Moon, P. **A Bibliography of Jazz Discographies.** London: British Institute of Jazz Studies, 1970.

0492   Sheatsley, P. B. "A Quarter Century of Jazz Discography." *Record Research*, 58 (February 1964), 3-6.

0493   Carey, David A. **Directory of Recorded Jazz and Swing Music.** Fordingbridge, Hampshire: Delphic Press, 1950– . ML156.4 J3 C3
        Duckles 67–1279; Duckles 74–1768

0494   Delaunay, Charles. **New Hot Discography: The Standard Directory of Recorded Jazz** . . . New York: Criterion, 1948. xviii, 608p. ML156.4 J3 D42
        Duckles 67–1280; Duckles 74–1769; Winchell 67–BH128

0495   **Jazz Discography.** Ed. Albert J. McCarthy. London: Cassell, 1958– . (annual). ML156.4 J3 J4
        Duckles 67–1283; Duckles 74–1778

0496   Rust, Brian. **Jazz Records, A–Z** . . . Middlesex: the Author, 1961– . ML156.4 J3 R9
        Duckles 67–1285
        In three volumes to date, covering 1897-1931 (1961), 1932-42 (1965), and 1942-67 (1968).

MISCELLANEOUS

These sources deal with diverse facets of recorded music. They are given in alphabetic sequence.

0497   Association for Recorded Sound Collections. **A Preliminary Directory of Sound Recordings Collections in the United States and Canada.** New York: New York Public Library, 1967. 157p. ML128 P28 A9
        Duckles 74–1818
        A list of important record collections and tape collections, by state (with Canada separately). Information: address, subjects of the collection, types of recordings held, size of the collection, availability of materials, references to literature. All sorts of musical and non-musical topics are found: e.g., swing 1935-50, piano rolls, the Mexican revolution. No indexes, unfortunately.

0498   **Collectors' Contact Guide, 1973-74.** Ed. Paul T. Jackson. Springfield, Ill.: Recorded Sound Research, 1973. 26p.
        Identifies over a hundred dealers and collectors for buying and selling of recordings, 20 magazines with auction lists or disc advertising, eight tape rental libraries, 15 directories and handbooks on recorded sound.

0499   Coover, James, and Richard Colvig. **Medieval and Renaissance Music on Long-Playing Records.** Detroit: Information Service, Inc., 1964.

xii, 122p. (Detroit Studies in Music Bibliography, 6). Supplement: 1962-71. Detroit: Information Coordinators, Inc., 1973. 258p. (Detroit Studies in Music Bibliography, 26). ML156.2 C67

Duckles 67—1260; Duckles 74—1739; ARBA 74—1098

Base volume covered 387 items; supplement adds 459. All are analyzed and carefully organized, in sections by title, composer, and performer. The 1973 supplement also carries corrections and additions for the 1964 volume.

0500   Limbacher, James L. **Theatrical Events: A Selected List of Musical and Dramatic Performances on Long-Playing Records.** 5th ed. Dearborn, Mich.: Dearborn Public Library, 1968. 95p. (mimeographed).

Title list of plays, musicals, operettas, comedy routines, etc., with dates, disc information, and performers. Composer index. Author advises that this is "being readied in book form by Pierian Press."

0501   Murrells, Joseph. **Daily Mail Book of Golden Discs: The Story of Every Million Selling Disc in the World since 1903.** Ed. Norris and Ross McWhirter . . . London: McWhirter Twins on behalf of the Daily Mail, 1966. x, 374p. ML156.2 M87

More than 1,000 discs from eleven countries are discussed, in year-by-year sequence, from Caruso's "Vesti la Giubba" of 1903 to such 1965 winners as "Whipped Cream and Other Delights" by the Tijuana Brass. Background on performers, market data. Various statistical tables—e.g., "most million-selling discs" (Elvis Presley had 50 of them, the Beatles 37); "most discs sold" (Bing Crosby ahead with 250,000,000); best selling songs ("White Christmas" first) and songwriters (Fats Domino); etc., etc. Except for the Caruso, these golden sounds are all pop/jazz/rock.

0502   New York Library Association. Children's and Young Adult Services Section. **Recordings for Children: A Selected List** . . . 2d ed. New York: New York Public Library, Office of Children's Services, 1964. (1st ed. 1961). 43p. ML156.4 C5 N5

Winchell 67—BH133

All sorts of recommended discs: music, folk songs, stories, poems, games, and documentaries.

0503   Smolian, Steven. **A Handbook of Film, Theater and Television Music on Record, 1948-69.** New York: Record Undertaker, 1970. ML156.4 M6 S6

Duckles 74—1783

Consists of two booklets: first is an alphabetical title list with issue dates; second is an index by label and composer.

INDEX OF AUTHORS, TITLES,
AND SELECTED SUBJECTS

For author and title approaches, this index is intended to be complete: it accounts for all works referred to in the text, and it identifies editors, translators, series, etc. However, subject treatment is limited to a certain few topics that are not illuminated by the arrangement of entries in the book. Cumulative subject and classified indexes for Volumes 1 and 2 are planned for the second volume.

McWhirter, Norris. *Guinness Book of World Records*, 0164
McWhirter, Ross. *Guinness Book of World Records*, 0164
Madrid. Biblioteca Nactional. *Catálogo musical de la Biblioteca Nacional de Madrid,* por Higinio Anglés y José Subirá, 0383
Maier, Jul. Jos. *Die Musikalischen Handschriften . . .* (Munich), 0413
Mala encyklopedia hudby, 0198
Mala encyklopedia muzyki, 0034
Maleady, Antoinette. *Record and Tape Reviews Index . . .* [1971 and 1972], 0485
Malm, William P. *Music Cultures of the Pacific, the Near East, and Asia*, 0103
Mandyczewski, Eusebius. "Bücher und Schriften über Musik. Druckwerke und Handschriften aus der Zeit bis zum Jahre 1800," 0252
Mantuani, Joseph. *Tabulae codicum manuscriptorum praeter graecos et orientales in Bibliotheca Palatina Vindobonensi asservatorum . . .*, 0417
Manuel du libraire et de l'amateur de livres (Brunet), 0244
Manuscripts of Polyphonic Music (ca. 1320-1400) (Reaney), 0419
Manuscripts of Polyphonic Music: 11th-Early 14th Century (Reaney), 0419
"March, 1901, Catalog of Edison 'Concert' Cylinders," (Walsh), 0469
Marconi, Joseph. *Indexed Periodicals*, 0315
Martí, Samuel. *Alt-Amerika: Musik der Indianer in präkolumbischer Zeit*, 0119
Mary Flagler Cary Music Collection (Pierpont Morgan Library. New York), 0415
Masters Abstracts: Abstracts of Selected Masters Theses on Microfilm, 0342
Masters' Theses in Musicology, 0344
Mattheson, Johann. *Grundlage einer Ehren-Pforte, woran der tüchtigsten Capellmeister, Componisten, Musikgelehrten, Tonkünstler, etc. Leben, Wercke, Verdienste, etc. erscheinen sollen . . .*, 0199
Mededelingenblad ver nederlandse musikgeschichte, 0320
Medieval and Renaissance Music on Long-Playing Records (Coover and Colvig), 0499

Medieval Polyphony in the Bodleian Library, by Dom Anselm Hughes (Oxford. Bodleian Library), 0414
Memorable Days in Music (Cullen), 0161
Mendel, Hermann. *Musikalisches Conversations-Lexikon, eine Encyclopädie der gesammten musikalischen Wissenschaften . . .*, 0079
Mercer, Frank. *A General History of Music, from the Earliest Times to the Present Period* (Burney), 0096
Merseburger, Carl. *Kurzgefasstes Tonkünstlerlexikon für Musiker und Freunde der Musik . . .*, 0200
Mersmann, Hans. *Die Moderne Musik seit der Romantik*, 0095
Meyer, Andre. *Collection musicale André Meyer*, 0127
Meyer, Kathi. *Katalog der Musikbibliothek Paul Hirsch*, 0231
Meyers Enzyklopädisches Lexikon in 25 Bänden, p. 25
Meysel, Anton, 0258
MGG (Die Musik in Geschichte und Gegenwart: Allgemeine Enzyklopadie der Musik), 0058
Michaud, p. 54
Michel, François. *Encyclopédie de la musique*, 0072
Microfilm Abstracts, 0331
Middle East and North Africa, p. 54
Mies, Paul. *Musik im Umkreis der Kulturgeschichte. Ein Tabellenwerk aus der Geschichte der Musik, Literatur, bildenden Künste, Philosophie und Politik Europas*, 0110
Milan. Conservatorio de Musica "Giuseppe Verdi." Biblioteca. *Catalogo della biblioteca. Letteratura musicale e opere teoriche. Parte prima: Manoscritti e stampe fino al 1899*, 0232
Miller, Allan. *Historical Atlas of Music: A Comprehensive Study of the World's Music, Past and Present* (Collaer and Linden), 0160
Miscellaneous Manuscripts, 0425
Mitjana, Rafael. *Catalogue critique et descriptif des imprimés de musique des XVIe et XVIIe siècles . . .* (Uppsala), 0438
Mize, J. T. H. *International Who Is Who in Music*, 0138
MLA Index Series, 0210, 0330
Moderne Musik seit der Romantik (Mersmann), 0095
Mokry, Ladislav, 0198
Monatshefte für Musikgeschichte, 17. Jhg., Beilage, 0278